MASTERPIECES OF
CANADIAN ART
FROM THE NATIONAL
GALLERY OF CANADA

MASTERPIECES OF CANADIAN ART FROM THE NATIONAL GALLERY OF CANADA

DAVID BURNETT
FOREWORD BY DR. SHIRLEY L. THOMSON

Hurtig Publishers

Hurtig Publishers Ltd.
1302 Oxford Tower
10235–101 Street
Edmonton, Alberta
Canada T5J 3G1

Canadian Cataloguing in Publication Data

Burnett, David.
    Masterpieces of Canadian art from the
National Gallery of Canada

    ISBN 0-88830-344-0

    1. Art, Canadian.   2. Art, Modern—20th
century—Canada.   3. Art—Ontario—Ottawa.
4. National Gallery of Canada.   I. National
Gallery of Canada. · II. Title.
N6540.B87 1990   709′.71′07471   C90-091304-5

Printed and bound in Canada

Credits

All illustrations are from the National Gallery of Canada, except the following:

Art Gallery of Ontario, 124, 180, 204
Beaverbrook Art Gallery, 26, 60
Confederation Centre of the Arts, 54
Hamilton Art Gallery, 63
McCord Museum of Canadian History, 47
McMichael Canadian Art Collection, 112
Richard Robitaille, Musée du Québec, 27

© 1990 for the works of Alex Colville (*Hound in Field*), Greg Curnoe, Yves Gaucher, Guido Molinari, Jean-Paul Riopelle, Claude Tousignant, and Joyce Wieland, obtained through VISART Copyright Inc.

    Every effort has been made to obtain necessary copyright permissions and to attribute all sources correctly, both textual and pictorial. The author will welcome any information that will allow the correction of any omissions or errors.

Contents

Foreword

In May 1988 the National Gallery of Canada moved into a splendid new building. The gallery was founded in 1880, but only now do we have a museum designed and built to house our national collections of art. The curators have used the gallery's magnificent spaces and natural lighting to show the works to their best advantage, and our many visitors, from Canada and abroad, agree that the Canadian collection shines as never before.

I was delighted when Mel Hurtig suggested a book on the ''masterpieces'' in the Canadian collection, a book which would be both an introduction and a guide to some of our finest works. Dr. David Burnett selected the images and wrote the text of the book. Identifying ''masterpieces'' was no doubt a daunting task, since we all have our favourites in the collection. But it seemed to me interesting and appropriate that the book, designed for visitors and interested readers, should be written by someone who was himself a visitor, rather than being part of the gallery staff.

I believe Dr. Burnett has succeeded in distilling the essence of the Canadian collection, and the book's fine reproductions and informative text will give pleasure to both the visitor and the reader at home. I know they will enjoy these paintings as much as I do.

Dr. Shirley L. Thomson, Director,
National Gallery of Canada

National Gallery of Canada, south elevation.

Introduction

"Masterpiece" is now an open term—simple to declare, impossible to define, and always subject to dispute. Its original meaning, however, was very specific; a *meesterstuk* in Dutch or a *meisterstück* in German was the individual work by which a craftsman was judged qualified to pursue his trade. With the evolution from the guild system into the academies of fine art, election to the academy, which carried important career advantages, required presentation of a work. Even today, election to the Royal Canadian Academy requires an artist to present a diploma work. This practice has had a special place in the development of the National Gallery collections. The founding of the gallery was a direct result of the establishment of the Royal Canadian Academy two years earlier. The gallery opened with a collection of twenty-five works, all but one of them the diploma pieces of the first group of academicians.

The original meaning of "masterpiece" thus barely survives. Now it tends to be used in two different ways. Precisely, it identifies *the* very best work from an artist's career. More generally and more commonly, it designates *a* major or significant work, so that there may be a number of "masterpieces" within an artist's output. It is in this broad sense that I have chosen to highlight specific artistic achievements which I feel are of masterpiece status.

In making the selection for *Masterpieces of Canadian Art from the National Gallery of Canada*, I kept several factors in mind. First, the National Gallery houses the largest and most significant collection of Canadian art. In wanting to show how this represents the story of Canadian art, I sought a chronological balance—the larger number of examples from the modern period reflects the greater range and quantity of activity in comparison to earlier times. Second, my selection was based partly on the contribution that individual artists have made to art in Canada. Lucius O'Brien or William Raphael, for instance, would not rank as innovative artists if weighed in a European context, but their achievements in setting standards and giving direction to art in Canada were most substantial. In later periods it was the strength of regional developments that gave art in Canada its particular character, while in recent years, with the growing internationalism in art, the horizon of expectation for Canadian art has expanded accordingly.

Significant though the National Gallery's collections are, they are not all-inclusive. This is particularly notable in the limited representation of important works from the early period in Quebec. The reasons for this reflect a complex historical situation. The most important early patron of the arts was the Roman Catholic Church, and the major surviving works are in Quebec museums or ecclesiastical collections. Further, it was quite some years after the National Gallery was founded that it gained independence from the artists' societies and was able to assert its full responsibility as a national museum of art. The Act of Parliament constituting the National Gallery was only passed in 1913, the same year that the gallery gained its first director, Eric Brown. Gradually, the process of developing the collections on a historical basis was established, though it was only in the late 1920s that the first early Quebec art was acquired.

National Gallery of Canada,
interior of Canadian Galleries.

The National Gallery now collects across the broad range of Canadian art in both the contemporary and historical areas. Yet the collections inevitably reflect the priorities of the curators. Their decisions have been particularly difficult in contemporary areas, partly because of the range of possibilities and partly because the acquisitions made today in so influential an institution as the National Gallery become images for the future—art history is being made. Some twentieth-century artists have been represented by relatively minor paintings or have been omitted altogether. However, there has been an active search for important works to fill such gaps. Thus, although some gaps still remain to be filled, I have been able to include major works from the 1950s and 1960s by Ronald Bloore, Jock Macdonald, William Ronald, Yves Gaucher, and Harold Town which have been added to the collection in the past few years. Even so, my selection can serve as no more than a foretaste of the cornucopia of art displayed in the gallery. There are some ten thousand works of Canadian art in the National Gallery. This book illustrates just over one percent of them.

An even more important development than the new acquisitions has been a change in the way the works are displayed. With the opening of the new building in 1988, the richness and range of the collections can be seen for the first time, and under excellent conditions. Moshe Safdie's sensitivity to the purpose of the building when designing the National Gallery has resulted in a range of spaces finely attuned to the particular forms of the works displayed. To move from room to room is to be impressed by the sense of an unfolding heritage.

The Artists
and Their
Masterpieces

Thomas Davies

c.1737–1812

In Canada's early years, there were two powerful influences on the development of artistic activity: the Roman Catholic Church and the British army. Whereas the church had been the principal patron of the arts in New France, in the English communities it was the army that provided the stimulus. Officer training at the Royal Military Academy in Woolwich, England, included instruction in drawing and watercolour painting so that the men would be able to make topographical records. For the most part, the work these men produced was, at best, of pedestrian competence, but there were a few officers whose personal interests, allied with natural talent, allowed them to develop their rudimentary training into work of individual style and aesthetic interest. In the later eighteenth century, the manner of such work was invariably the Picturesque approach to landscape painting that was given popular currency through the writings of the Rev. William Gilpin. The Picturesque became so much a part of a civilized, visual education that it came to appear a "natural" way to see landscape.

Thomas Davies was one of the earliest of the British army watercolour painters in Canada. In many respects he was the most interesting. He arrived in Halifax in 1757 as a lieutenant in the artillery and spent the next few years taking part in various campaigns. He seems to have had three more spells of duty in North America, including participation in the American War of Independence. On his last appointment in Canada, between 1786 and 1790, he was based in Quebec. He enjoyed success in the army, retiring with the rank of lieutenant-general. Through all this time, probably more for personal satisfaction than military purposes, he sketched and painted. His earliest known drawings date from his first Canadian tour, but his finest work was done in the late 1780s, and it is on the basis of this that his importance to the development of Canadian art is measured. This reputation is of relatively recent date, for it was only in 1953 that a portfolio of his watercolours from the 1780s was discovered in the library of the Earl of Derby. Twenty of these works were acquired by the National Gallery in 1954.

The popularity of Gilpin's notion of the Picturesque arose from its combining contemporary interests in topography with an aesthetic that viewed nature as an ordered and largely benevolent force. Gilpin doubted that "America" would yield much in the way of Picturesque subjects because the land was so vast and the impact of human intervention so limited. Davies's approach responded broadly to the Picturesque, but in a special sense that grew in importance towards the end of the century, the sense that valued the exotic and unusual.

Most of the army topographical painters used the watercolour medium primarily as a way of colour washing or tinting their drawings, but Davies used the medium essentially as a painting medium, building tonal structure with it and disposing a broad range of rich colour. *A View on the River La Puce near Quebec, North America* of 1789 is characteristic of these full-bodied pictures. The style is naive: we search in vain for a unified sense of light; the development of perspective is idiosyncratic; his handling of the rushing river is charmingly rather than naturalistically organized; and his figure drawing is awkward. But where Davies's work gains strength is in the way he expresses his sense of wonder at the untamed setting. Rather than trying to impose on the land a style that had been developed to represent European landscapes, Davies gives emphasis to what makes the Canadian scenes unique—the density of the forests, the power of the rivers, the exotic fauna, and a sense of colour in the trees and sky that was quite different from that experienced by most Europeans. Whereas later and more technically accomplished painters would depict the Canadian scene, many would fail to match Davies's acute expression of his reaction to an abundant new land.

Thomas Davies
A View on the River La Puce near Quebec, North America (1789),
watercolour over graphite on wove paper, 34.1 × 51.6 cm.
Purchase, 1954.
Accession No. 6282.

George Heriot

1759–1839

The notion of the amateur—a development of the late eighteenth century—reflected the belief that a cultivated person was one who had practical accomplishments in the arts as well as an educated appreciation of them. Such practical endeavour was essentially conservative in taste and conventional in style. Particularly favoured in Britain was the Picturesque landscape, the origins of which lay in the work of such seventeenth-century painters as Claude Lorrain and Nicolas Poussin, and which depended on transforming and heightening reality for aesthetic effect. It was an approach often combined with the contemporary interest in the topography. George Heriot was such an amateur, a prolific watercolorist whose work survives in collections in Canada, the United States, and Europe.

For nearly twenty-five years, Heriot worked in the British administration of Lower Canada in Quebec City. A Scot, educated in Edinburgh, he spent four years in the West Indies, 1777–81, and then went to England where, like Thomas Davies, he attended the Royal Military College. There he studied with Paul Sandby, who taught the cadets drawing and watercolour painting for topographical purposes. In 1792 Heriot was posted to Quebec, where he served as clerk of the cheque in the Ordnance Department until 1800. With the support of William Pitt the Younger, he was then appointed to the influential job of deputy postmaster general. This office involved Heriot in a considerable amount of travel. We know that he went to Halifax and as far westward as Sandwich, near Detroit. He was in York (Toronto) several times, and he viewed Niagara Falls and went at least once to the United States. He took his painting materials on his trips and made small wash sketches, which he later worked up into watercolours.

From his earliest works in the 1780s, Heriot showed himself to be a competent draughtsman and facile watercolorist in the manner of Sandby. During a period of home leave in 1796–97, he seems to have studied the most recent examples of the watercolour art in England, because his work from the turn of the century shows a new fluency and lightness of manner. In 1804 he

published *The History of Canada* and in 1807 an illustrated book, *Travels Through the Canadas*, which proved popular. Reflecting his background at the Royal Military College and the contemporary interest in travel and exploration, Heriot's work is topographically significant. Apart from his "views," he also made a group of watercolours of the Huron at Jeune Lorette. (It was popular to make expeditions from Quebec to observe dances and ceremonies at nearby native villages.)

The topographical interest of Heriot's work is expressed in a Picturesque style, the latter aspect predominating in his finest pieces, such as *Lake St. Charles near Quebec* of *c.*1801. This watercolour ultimately reflects the structure and lyricism of Claude Lorrain's landscapes: the central feature of a green and a russet tree, the *repoussoir* effects of foliage that define the foreground, and an open view across the middle ground leading to softly painted, blue mountains in the background. His handling of the watercolour has a smooth touch, generating a fine sense of light in the foreground trees and a well-balanced development of atmospheric effects that give a convincing command of space.

Heriot's stay in Quebec came to an abrupt end in 1816. For some years, he had been in conflict with the various military and civilian authorities as a result of his intransigent administration of the mail service. Matters came to a head with the appointment of Sir Gordon Drummond as administrator of the two Canadas, and Heriot appears to have felt it wise to resign and return to England. In retirement, he continued both to paint and travel—it would seem that he enjoyed a private income—and there are watercolours of wide-ranging sites in Britain and Europe dating into the 1830s.

George Heriot
Lake St. Charles near Quebec (*c.*1801),
watercolour over graphite on laid paper, 27.3 × 44.5 cm.
Purchase, 1954.
Accession No. 6320.

William Berczy, Sr.

*c.*1744–1813

What makes *The Woolsey Family* such a special document? It is not that the family was especially prominent—John Woolsey was a respected and successful businessman but not a major public figure—nor that William Berczy was an exceptional or influential painter. The form of the painting belongs to a well-established tradition, the "conversation piece," which had become a popular type of family-portrait genre in Europe since its development in the late 1720s. This picture, however, was an innovation for Canada and an important personal statement by both the painter and the man who commissioned it; it was an assertion of their achievements, a declaration of status and future prospects. Berczy wrote to his wife soon after meeting Woolsey: "My works, dependent as they are on the gentle muse who is our friend and support, are taking a most advantageous turn."*

William Berczy was sixty-three when he went to Quebec to meet John Woolsey. Born in Saxony, he was brought up in Vienna, where his father was a diplomat. At the time of his marriage in 1785, he was described as a "miniaturist"; he exhibited at the Royal Academy in London in 1790 and drew a portrait of George III the following year. He then set painting to one side for some years and became a land agent, recruiting Germans to settle in New York State. This proved to be a star-crossed adventure, though he eventually found land in Upper Canada for his group of settlers. His problems continued when he returned to England, where he was imprisoned for debt, but in 1801 he was back in Canada, first in York (Toronto) and then, in 1804, in Montreal. At this point, he seems to have put all his efforts back into his artistic work. It was probably Judge Panet of Montreal who recommended Berczy to John Woolsey, but the artist's hopes that the success of the Woolsey picture would lead to further important commissions in Quebec were not realized. In the last years of his life, Berczy attempted to find a publisher for his extensive writings. He was in New York for this purpose in 1813 when he died.

John Woolsey was born in Quebec in 1767. His father, a merchant, had come over from Ireland a few years earlier and married Marie-Josephette Trefflé Rottot. Woolsey went into business and in 1797 married Julie Lemoine Despins of Montreal. They had four children: William Darley, born 1799; William Henry, born 1803; Eleonora, born 1805; and John Bryan, born 1808.

Commissioning a family portrait entailed a significant financial commitment, particularly for full-length figures. Berczy charged £10 for each of the eight figures, adding nothing to his bill for the dog. Woolsey had originally contracted for a painting of seven people (himself, his wife and children, and his brother-in-law, Benjamin Lemoine), but a few days later the agreement was changed to add an eighth person, Woolsey's mother, who had apparently been forgotten.

Berczy expected the work to take him three or four months, but it was almost a year before the painting was finished. John Woolsey stands presiding over his family. They are posed in a spacious, well-proportioned room with a fine view over the gardens of the Hôtel-Dieu de Québec and across the St. Lawrence to the Île d'Orléans and Cap Tourmente. It is the painting of a successful man who, with his growing family, looks forward with confidence to the future. But this representation is a poignant one, for only one person in the picture outlived him; this was his brother-in-law. Woolsey's second son, William Henry, was drowned at the age of fifteen; William Darley died of pleurisy when he was twenty-six, soon after entering the Grand Séminaire; and Eleonora died at twenty-three of consumption. Woolsey's wife also died of consumption, in 1840, and six years later his youngest son, John Bryan, died of a liver disease. Woolsey's mother had died in 1826. In 1848 Woolsey listed out this sad history and glued it to the back of the painting.

The charm of the painting lies both in the pride of the client and in the ambition of the artist to make a major picture linked to the European fashion. The painting is firmly structured, the space generously developed, and the relationship between the room and the landscape outside is well handled. There are some awkward passages—the perspective of the table and young Mrs. Woolsey's chair, and the proportions of Woolsey's left arm—but Berczy has sympathetically caught the character of the family: the freedom of the younger children, the withdrawn studiousness of William Darley, the posed elegance of Benjamin Lemoine, and the self-conscious informality of the other adults. It is a picture of the Woolsey family, and yet, more broadly, it is a picture of "family," special in its ordinariness.

*Jean Trudel, *William Berczy: The Woolsey Family. Masterpieces in the National Gallery of Canada*, No. 7 (Ottawa: National Gallery, 1976), p.18.

William Berczy, Sr.
The Woolsey Family (1809),
oil on canvas, 59.8 × 87.2 cm.
Gift of Major Edgar C. Woolsey, Ottawa, 1952.
Accession No. 5875.

Louis Dulongpré

1759–1843

Major art in New France had, for the most part, been made under the patronage of the Catholic Church: altarpieces, decorative work, portraits of priests and nuns, devotional objects. Many of the artists were themselves clerics, and some had been sent over by their Order from France—Frère Luc (1614–85) being the most accomplished. The demand for art in secular society grew more slowly, for it depended on a certain level of wealth and sophistication being reached in communities with a range of educated people. The point of reference remained, directly or indirectly, metropolitan France; but it is interesting to trace the emergence of self-awareness in a new society, a self-awareness in the patronage of art, which found its most significant secular expression in portraiture.

Our knowledge of artists working in Quebec into the early nineteenth century remains quite limited, and numerous problems of attribution remain. In part this is because the popular style of portraiture tended to follow conventional lines, setting constraints on the range of an individual artist's expression. The primary concern of the patrons would have been a good (and favourable) likeness and the presentation of a dignified bearing suitable to their station. They would not have been much interested, nor pleased, with "interpretative" renderings; an artist attempting such could not have looked forward to enjoying an abundance of work.

By contemporary accounts, a lack of work was never a problem for Louis Dulongpré. According to various sources, he is credited with having made between three and four thousand portraits in oil or pastel. Over a career of, say, some thirty or forty years, this would have meant one portrait every three days and the patronage of a measurable percentage of the population of Montreal. What we know of Dulongpré is that his interests were broader and more extensive than just portrait painting. He was born on the outskirts of Paris and, by his own account, he studied at "the best academies." It would seem that he went first to the American colonies during the War of Independence, moving to Montreal in the mid-1780s. His accomplishments, in addition to painting, have been variously listed as musician, topographer, and theatre manager. As a painter, he is said to have painted theatre sets and to have worked in various churches, notably painting the ceiling of Notre-Dame in Montreal (destroyed in the 1820s) as well as fulfilling his commissions as a portraitist.

Dulongpré's portrait of *Joseph Papineau* of 1825 was not only of a seigneur and a member of the Legislative Assembly, but also of a friend: the two men, much of an age, were in the habit of playing chess and backgammon together. The painting is a conventional half-length, with Papineau seated at a desk; books line the back wall, while other books and a couple of quill pens stand close at hand. Although the description of the features is simplified, the painting makes a sympathetic impression, and we can imagine the sittings having been carried out in an informal atmosphere.

The stretcher of the painting is inscribed with the name "Joseph Papineau" and "Property of GC Dessaulles." Papineau's daughter Rosalie married into the Dessaulles family, and a document originally attached to the back of the picture further identifies the sitter and notes that he was the father of Madame Rosalie Dessaulles and Louis-Joseph Papineau, the nationalist politician who led the Parti Canadien, later the Parti Patriote.

Louis Dulongpré
Joseph Papineau (1825),
oil on canvas, 76.4 × 60.9 cm.
Purchase, 1974.
Accession No. 18022.

9

Robert Field

*c.*1769–1819

Halifax was the creation of British colonial ambition and its sustaining military presence. Established in 1749 as a counter to the French fort at Louisbourg, the town enjoyed the growth associated with its strategic importance in the wars that ended with Napoleon's defeat in 1815. The garrison and naval facilities, as well as the influx of Loyalists from the United States, gave Halifax a sizable population of educated people who had lived in larger cities and who set out to create an acceptable social ambience. A major boost, both to the physical and the social structure of Halifax, came during the six years beginning in 1794, when Prince Edward, Duke of Kent, commanded the garrison. The army and naval officers, senior officials, and prosperous businessmen established such institutions as the exclusive Rockingham Club and the Halifax Chess, Pencil and Brush Club. The latter, which was Canada's first art club, was founded around 1787 and flourished for some thirty years.

A manifestation of fashionable life was the demand for portraits. For Haligonians, this often meant going to the United States to find artists of acceptable quality who were *au fait* with the current manners. It was evidently in response to a need that Robert Field, who had been painting portraits for a number of years in Baltimore, Philadelphia, Washington, and Boston, went to Halifax in 1808. He had the right connections, painting the lieutenant-governor, Sir George Prevost, and the previous lieutenant-governor, Sir John Wentworth, that first year. Introductions to the Rockingham Club members continued to keep Field well supplied with work over the next eight years.

Field was in his late thirties when he arrived in Halifax. Trained at the Royal Academy schools in London, he had moved to the United States in 1794. He was acquainted with Gilbert Stuart, once a pupil of Benjamin West and since the early 1790s one of the most successful American portrait painters. (Stuart's

style reflected the informal naturalism of George Romney and Henry Raeburn, and his reputation was assured by the rare privilege of having George Washington sit for him. Copies of his Washington portraits were in great demand, and it is possible that Field was among the artists who made copies.) Field remained in Halifax until 1816, by which time he had probably exhausted the market in a city whose prosperity suffered with the ending of the Napoleonic Wars. He moved to Kingston, Jamaica, also a major British military and administrative centre, and died there three years later from yellow fever.

The *Lieutenant Provo William Parry Wallis, R.N.*, was painted around 1813. In type and approach it is typical of the portraits of the day, established in the tradition of Reynolds and Gainsborough and the more recent developments introduced by Romney, but looking forward to the Romantic portraiture of Raeburn and Thomas Lawrence. Field was in no way an innovator, but he was an accomplished master of his genre. His work has an easy, painterly quality—loose in the stormy background of the sky, exact in the detail of Wallis's uniform, sensitive in rendering the features of the young man's face. If the painting lacks conviction as to the individuality of character, it fulfils the expectations for a sympathetic likeness, aiding nature's endowments and asserting the subject's social standing. This was Field's forte, and he introduced a standard of professional quality to the isolated "polite" society of early nineteenth-century Halifax.

Robert Field
Lieutenant Provo William Parry Wallis, R.N. (1813),
oil on canvas, 76.2 × 63.5 cm.
Purchase, 1950.
Accession No. 5057.

11

Joseph Légaré

1795–1855

Montreal's dominance of painting in the late eighteenth and early nineteenth centuries came under challenge from Quebec through the work of a remarkable trio of artists—Joseph Légaré, Antoine-Sébastien Plamondon, and Théophile Hamel—who were linked by a successive master-pupil relationship. Through their ambition and the quality of their work, they brought Quebec pride of place in the course of the nineteenth century.

Légaré came from a wealthy Quebec family and his interest in art was developed from an early age. There are few facts, though several conflicting stories, about his artistic training. The most plausible account has Légaré remaining in Quebec and, in effect, undertaking his own training by studying older works of art. That he was able to do this was the result of an ambitious step he took as a young man, an action with important consequences both for him and for art in Canada.

In the upheavals that swept through France during the French Revolution, vast amounts of fixed and movable property belonging to the church and the nobility were seized or sold, and speculators were often able to buy at desperately low prices. In the years after the revolution, two French priests, brothers by the name of Desjardins, acquired a large collection of paintings from one such speculator. Louis-Joseph Desjardins sold nearly two hundred European pictures, dating from the sixteenth to eighteenth centuries, in Quebec between 1817 and 1820. Légaré purchased a large number of these pictures at auction and then cleaned and restored them. Later, he converted his studio into an art gallery to display these and other European works alongside his own paintings, thus establishing the first Canadian art gallery. Unfortunately, the level of connoisseurship involved in the Desjardins Collection was low (or the level of duplicity high); many of the paintings which had generous attributions have since been revealed to be copies, and others were the work of minor artists. Nevertheless, the collection provided a stock of images that were representative of the European tradition; and Légaré, who continued to add to his collection throughout his lifetime, did a good business in making copies of the paintings. After his death, many of the pictures were acquired by Université Laval.

Légaré gained a reputation for political activism—he was an ardent supporter of the Patriotes and Louis-Joseph Papineau, and was arrested during the 1837 Rebellion simply for his known views. This enthusiasm also influenced his art, for his immersion in the European tradition through his knowledge of the Desjardins Collection was joined with a concern to make the Canadian experience central to his work. Many of his landscapes show a direct response to the land, and he made a striking group of urban pictures relating to contemporary events; for instance, of the cholera plagues of the 1830s and the great fire of 1845 which destroyed the Saint-Roch district of Quebec. His contribution was already recognized by 1828 when the Montreal Society for the Encouragement of Arts and Sciences in Canada awarded him a medal and described him as Canada's first "historical painter."

This rare combination of Légaré's knowledge of the European tradition and his desire to give expression to his own time and place is exemplified in the sensitivity of his portrait of Josephte Ourné, which dates from around 1840. The painting is striking for its period in that it does not treat the native woman as a curiosity, but portrays her as an individual living within a particular context. The background of the painting is of the forest and water, representing not merely a setting but the world in and by which she lived. The fish and bird she has caught reveal her way of life as united with the land. And the way in which Légaré has painted her clothing and jewellery gives them the same emphasis that he gave in portraits of the wives of Quebec merchants, dressed up in the finery that marked their place in the context of their society. Finally, he has held for us the expression of a particular person, an expression of suspicion mixed with pride.

Joseph Légaré
Josephte Ourné (c.1840),
oil on canvas, 131.5 × 95.5 cm.
Purchase, 1975.
Accession No. 18309.

Antoine-Sébastien Plamondon

1804–1895

Antoine-Sébastien Plamondon became something of a Quebec institution, asserting a pre-eminent position both by the quality of his art and his aggressive behaviour towards potential competitors. With the exception of four years studying in Europe, Plamondon, the pupil of Légaré and the master of Hamel, lived his ninety-two years in or near Quebec City. Although he became founding vice-president of the Royal Canadian Academy in 1880 and continued painting into his eightieth year, Plamondon did his best work in the 1830s and 1840s. In 1851 he moved to Neuville, living the life of a gentleman-farmer and painting when it pleased him.

Plamondon was apprenticed to Légaré in 1819, and much of his practical training came from restoring paintings from the Desjardins brothers' collection. In 1826, with support from the church, he went to Paris and studied under Jean-Baptiste Paulin Guérin, a minor classical portrait painter. Apart from a few pictures in other genres, Plamondon's work took two main directions: religious paintings for Quebec churches, and portraits for the socially prominent of the city. Most of his religious paintings were copies or versions of existing works, including a number from the Desjardins Collection. This was skilled work—a contribution to a substantial, if largely unconsidered, aspect of the history of painting—but Plamondon's creative genius lay in his portraits.

Plamondon's finest moment was in 1841 when he made portraits of three young nuns of the Hôpital Général. Two of the paintings, *Soeur Saint-Joseph* and *Soeur Sainte-Anne*, are in the Musée de l'Hôpital Général; the third and the finest of them is *Soeur Saint-Alphonse*. The three young women came from well-placed Quebec families, who commissioned the portraits. Soeur Saint-Alphonse was born Marie-Louise Émilie Pelletier in 1816, the daughter of a prosperous merchant. When she was nineteen and entering the social whirl of Quebec, Plamondon painted a conventional, rather dull portrait of her. Three years later, having gained the reluctant permission of her father, she became a postulant for the choir at the Hôpital Général. She took her vows in 1839; she became choir mistress and also taught English and deportment. It seems that she always suffered poor health, and she died, probably from heart disease, in 1846.

The three 1841 portraits follow a similar form; the women are seated, half-turned to the right, and they gaze steadily off into the distance. They wear the Augustinian habit—Sister Sainte-Anne still with the novitiate's white veil—and a silver pectoral cross. Each holds a book in her right hand, one finger marking a page as if she had just paused in her devotional reading, and each portrait is set against a plain background, carefully modulated to enhance the figure and produce a convincing illusion of space.

The subject is a demanding one for the portrait painter. Colour is limited; but the voluminous habits of black and white comprise a range of textures and materials—muslin, linen, wool—loose and deeply folded here, starched and tight there. A convincing likeness is made difficult by the enclosure of the face by linen bands; but in contrast to Plamondon's cliché portrait of the young Marie-Louise Pelletier (soft features, sweet charm, rosebud lips, and smiling, innocent eyes), in *Soeur Saint-Alphonse* he responds to a young woman of character. There is structure in her face, and the distant gaze of her eyes and the set of her mouth, slightly flexed at its corners, express a confidence and inner calm. Her tranquillity belies the subtle hints of weariness and the strains of ill health in the deep-shadowed setting of her eyes and the contrast between the pallor of her face and her blushed cheeks.

A contemporary writer, lavishing praise on the nuns' portraits, pointed out how there were no visible brushstrokes: "This is another secret of the accomplished artist, who unveils the picture before your eyes, revealing nothing but Nature." For, he said, painters "strive to eradicate the traces of their labours, to show only what is natural, free, for Nature in all its manifestations is free and without constraint."* In Paris, when Plamondon was studying there, "revealing nothing but Nature" was gaining a very different interpretation in the paintings of Géricault and the early books of Balzac. Plamondon held to the classical tradition, but he transcended its constraints in *Soeur Saint-Alphonse* and gave us a sensitive and affecting reflection of the young woman's presence, without compromising the conventions suitable for the portrait of a nun.

*John R. Porter, *Antoine Plamondon: Soeur Saint-Alphonse. Masterpieces in the National Gallery of Canada, No. 4* (Ottawa: National Gallery, 1975), pp. 22–23.

Antoine Plamondon
Soeur Saint-Alphonse (1841),
oil on canvas, 90.6 × 72.0 cm.
Purchase, 1937.
Accession No. 4297.

Unknown Artist

19th Century

In general terms, art history has made a broad distinction between the work of professional or semi-professional artists and that of folk or naive artists. It is a distinction between two traditions: one based on historical development and academic training, the other spontaneous and unschooled. In reality, these traditions often touch or overlap; the work of the unknown painter of *Micmac Indians* is a case in point. The artist probably lived in one of the small, isolated communities of the Maritimes in the early years of the nineteenth century. He or she was not an amateur in the sense in which George Heriot was one, for Heriot had an appreciable knowledge of the mainstream of art. Nor was this unknown artist wholly naive, for the work reveals evidence of some training, albeit rudimentary, and an acquaintance with professional works of art.

By stylistic comparison, it is possible to identify two watercolours at the Beaverbrook Art Gallery as being by the same hand as *Micmac Indians*. These pictures are linked by formal similarities, related themes, details such as a varied range of wild and domestic animals, and a certain perception of native life. In comparison to, say, Henry Sandham's view of the spare and harsh conditions of Micmac life in his *Micmac Indian Camp, Gulf of St Lawrence* (National Gallery), this painter shows a life crammed with incident, centred on a firmly built birchbark wigwam, and with the hunt taking place from well-shaped canoes. The people are finely dressed and well supplied with muskets. Traps lie to one side of the wigwam; a toboggan and snowshoes are set out ready for the winter; and there is evidence of abundant game.

The painting is a delightful mixture of knowing and naivety. Many of the elements—the wigwam, canoes, and shorelines are strongly drawn and well modelled. Keeping everything firmly parallel to the picture plane overcomes some of the artist's limitations in perspectival drawing. The problems are most clearly apparent in the figures, particularly in trying to deal with the complex, pivoting actions of the people paddling the canoes. It is interesting that while the artist has sought naturalism in the figures, which end up looking awkward, there has been a decorative approach to depicting the flock of geese by finding an ingenious, emblematic way to express confusion, escape, and death among the birds.

The emphasis in the painting is on native people and the details of their daily life; they are given a scale of importance that makes the landscape of secondary interest. Yet the painting of the trees—the loosely brushed foliage and heavily textured trunks—and the gradations of colour in the sky and water show a control and appreciation of the handling of oil glazes that indicates some knowledge of technique and a study of more sophisticated paintings. In addition, the artist planned the composition with some care, setting the horizon exactly halfway up the picture and marking the midway point across the canvas by the tallest fir trees. To prevent this underlying structure from appearing too rigid, the artist has compensated by the way in which the bared trunks and branches echo each other across the picture, and the way their sharp, knurled forms play in formal counterpoint with the flock of geese.

We cannot pretend that this unknown artist is someone of rare originality. The charm of the picture lies in its confusion of the naive and academic traditions. Yet it has a strength in the direct way that it represents a people who, for centuries, have lived in balance with their surroundings—a sense of balance which this artist, whoever he or she may have been, could understand only as an observer.

Unknown artist
Micmac Indians (*c.*1850),
oil on canvas, 45.7 × 61.0 cm.
Purchase, 1957.
Accession No. 6663.

Robert Todd

1809–1866

The nineteenth century brought renewed interest to the debate over the distinctions between the fine arts and the decorative arts. To some, this was merely an enjoyable aesthetic and theoretical argument; but for the majority of artists, the reality of the issue was more prosaic: how to make a living from one's chosen craft. Some artists took the route of becoming specialists in a particular area—say, in portrait painting or stained-glass work—while others used their skills on a wide range of tasks, taking on whatever work they could find. For many, no matter in which area they worked, making a living meant joining the motley company of itinerant artists, who both in Europe and North America travelled from city to city in search of patrons.

In the first half of the nineteenth century only a handful of these itinerant artists made their way to Canada; there were few communities sufficiently substantial in population and social sophistication to support professional artists. We do not know why Robert Todd, as a man of twenty-five, chose to ply his trade in Quebec. He was born in Berwick-upon-Tweed in northeast England. We know nothing of his background or training, only that he arrived in Quebec in 1834, advertising himself as a "house, sign, carriage, and ornamental painter," and claiming to have worked for English and Scots gentry and nobility. In 1841 he issued another advertisement, adding figure carving and gilding to his skills, no doubt in the hope of attracting the significant patronage which the Catholic Church disposed. His clients, however, were more probably drawn from the English-speaking merchants of the city and officers from the garrison. The small number of easel paintings attributable to Todd were likely done as commissions from these people, who wanted souvenirs of Quebec.

Montmorency Falls, just outside Quebec, had long been a popular venue for both winter and summer excursions. Todd seems to have turned the picturesque setting into a popular image, because a number of paintings of this setting are recorded. The National Gallery painting, *The Ice Cone, Montmorency Falls*, of around 1850, is a charming and finely made picture, possibly commissioned by an army officer who wanted to have his two-horse sleigh recorded against the falls. Todd's approach to perspective and compositional organization reflects his skills as a decorator. One can see this in the precise way he outlines the figures, horses, and sleighs, and how all these features are held rigidly parallel to the picture plane, allowing him to play them against the curves of the hills and cliffs in the background.

The naivety of the picture is part of its decorative charm, a naivety residing not only in the stiffness of the composition but also in how Todd sought to unite two distinct categories of painting: genre, with the figures and animals in the foreground; and landscape in the background. It was an approach that Cornelius Krieghoff used with such success. It may be that the careers of the two men crossed, fatefully for Todd. Krieghoff moved to Quebec from Montreal in 1853, and that year or soon after Todd left Quebec for Toronto. Krieghoff brought with him the substantial reputation he had made in Montreal, and he was to raise it further during the ten years he spent in Quebec. There was clearly a market in Quebec for genre pictures in landscape settings, and it is tempting to believe that Todd realized that it would be Krieghoff, rather than he, who would benefit. Todd's move to Toronto, however, brought him little joy, and in 1861 he was complaining that "Toronto is too new and too poor to support an ornamental artist."*

*J. Russell Harper, *Painting in Canada: A History*, 2nd ed. (Toronto: University of Toronto Press, 1977), p.102.

Robert Todd
The Ice Cone, Montmorency Falls (*c*.1850),
oil on canvas, 34.3 × 45.9 cm.
Purchase, 1957.
Accession No. 6763.

Paul Kane

1810–1871

Paul Kane was the first Upper Canadian artist to gain wide public attention, catching the imagination of his contemporaries as he represented to them the vastness of the land and the character of its indigenous peoples and their cultures. His illustrated book, *Wanderings of an Artist among the Indians of North America*, published in London in 1859, proved most popular and went into three other language editions within four years. Kane was described in 1853, enthusiastically if not accurately, as the "first native artist in Canada"; he held one of the first one-man exhibitions in Canada and sold his most important series of paintings as a group for the handsome sum of $20,000.

Kane came to York (Toronto) as a boy around 1819 from his birthplace in County Cork, Ireland. Into his mid-thirties his career was undistinguished. After apprenticing as a decorative painter and taking drawing lessons, he worked as a furniture, sign, and house painter, and also accepted portrait commissions. Following a pattern common for the day, he spent a number of years as an itinerant artist, travelling to Detroit in 1836, then down to St. Louis, New Orleans, and Mobile. By 1841 he had accumulated sufficient funds for a European tour, which was considered essential for any serious artist. He went to Rome, Paris, and London, learning his craft and building his pictorial vocabulary by copying the Old Masters. In 1843 he was back in Mobile.

Kane returned to North America with a particular and driving ambition. While in London, he had seen an exhibition by the American painter George Catlin, depicting Indians and native life across the continent. Kane was inspired by Catlin's work and was determined to make a comprehensive record of Indian life. He returned to Toronto in 1845 and set out on a sketching expedition that took him to Lake Huron, Georgian Bay, Lake Michigan, and into Wisconsin. He returned to Toronto and painted up some of his sketches, which were shown at the first exhibition of the Toronto Society of Arts in 1847. Meanwhile, in 1846, he had set out on his second and most ambitious journey. Under the sponsorship of Sir George Simpson, governor of the Hudson's Bay Company, Kane travelled across the country, through Fort Garry to Fort Edmonton, and south to Fort Vancouver (now Vancouver, Washington State). He spent some months in that area and returned to Toronto in the fall of 1848. Within a few weeks he held a major exhibition of the sketches, which were to become the basis for the remainder of his life's work.

His most important project was a series of one hundred paintings recording his travels. He showed the first of these, to a great reception, at the 1851 provincial exhibition and completed the series in 1855. The following year he completed a dozen replicas, for which he had received government support; eleven were taken into the National Gallery in 1888 (one of the paintings having been destroyed by fire). The series of one hundred was bought by George Allan of Toronto and in 1912 was donated to the Royal Ontario Museum by Sir Edmund Osler, who had acquired it after Allan's death in 1901. Kane painted relatively little after 1856. His eyesight began to fail in 1859, and he closed his studio a few years later.

Kane's drawings and watercolours have a fine light-filled freshness, and his paintings are firmly structured and clearly drawn, precise but not overburdened with detail. In *White Mud Portage, Winnipeg River*, for instance, he sets a careful balance between the landscape and the activity around the river and portage. The form of the landscape and the manner in which it was painted adhere closely to the structure of European classical landscape, a type of painting that had been developed as suitable for uplifting themes on religious, mythological, and historical subjects. Kane's interest was to record cultures and ways of life that he realized were rapidly disappearing. There is a certain irony that his record of the indigenous cultures, which were under severe pressure from European settlement, should be expressed in a style that had been developed in European art to invoke a nostalgic view of its own mythic golden past.

Paul Kane
White Mud Portage, Winnipeg River (c.1851–56),
oil on canvas, 46.0 × 74.0 cm.
Transferred from the Parliament of Canada, 1888.
Accession No. 138.

Robert R. Whale

*c.*1807–1887

In the thirty-five years following the end of the Napole-onic Wars, the population of Upper Canada grew tenfold, to just under one million. This immigration, which was principally rural, saw the development of scores of small communities between the Ottawa Valley and the far southwest. Among the immigrants arriving in mid-century were a number of English artists, profes-sionals and semi-professionals; by settling in various parts of the colony, they established a broader base of artistic activity than the earlier generations of artists, who had been drawn to Toronto by the patronage of military and civilian society. Most of these newly arrived artists were minor figures who simply continued to paint the habitual English subjects in an English style. The few exceptions, both in terms of the quality of their work and their readiness to respond to their new surroundings, included Daniel Fowler, William Hind, and Robert Whale. Of the three, Whale was the least creatively talented, but his career is revealing in terms of the development of artistic activity in Canada's rural communities.

Whale was in his forties when he immigrated in 1852. He spent the remainder of his life in or near Brantford, with the exception of four years in the early 1870s when he went back to England. He was an enter-prising man, using his skills in ready response to the demands of the private market, but taking advantage of the limited opportunities for the public exhibition of art in Ontario. From 1847 on, the principal forum was the Upper Canada Provincial Exhibition. Held annually in a different centre each year, the exhibition was essentially an agricultural and craft fair with an "art" section. Until 1856, false teeth, among other items, were included in the "art" section. Absurd though this appears, it indi-cates how, among both the exhibition's organizers and audiences, painting was viewed merely as one of a number of skilled crafts. Whale and his two sons, who were also painters, used the exhibition vigorously and successfully to promote their work. They habitually entered the maximum number of works in every cate-gory, and they so consistently walked off with the prize

money as to cause resentment among other entrants. In another enterprising move, Whale painted a panorama of the 1857 Indian Mutiny and toured it around the province, charging an admission fee for viewing it.

Whale's principal work came from commissions for portraits and landscape paintings. He created a particu-larly popular image, showing a train travelling past Niagara Falls, and over the years a number of versions of this composition were made. (The National Gallery owns *The Canada Southern Railway at Niagara*, painted around 1870.) Whale was showing himself responsive to contemporary interests by combining two popular genres: an awe-inspiring aspect of the New World land-scape, and a "portrait" of one of the day's most progressive technical developments.

His most impressive individual painting is the *View of Hamilton*, made in 1853, shortly after his arrival in Canada. Canny as always, he has adapted one of the major traditions of landscape painting to the particular circumstances of his time and place. In broad terms, his approach to the landscape derives from the late-eigh-teenth-century English model established by Richard Wilson, who in turn took his influence from the great French master, Claude Lorrain. This model was of a broad and idealized view of nature—an eternally impressive but benign force—bathed in golden or rose-tinted light. Whale's commission obviously called for a topographical view of Hamilton, and he has combined this with a freely invented foreground. The scheme of the composition, with a group of trees off-centre allowing both a broad view and a restricted view into the distance, follows the long-established formula. Within this format, however, he has given the landscape a certain rawness—with the exposed rocks, the fallen and broken trees—to reconcile the ideal landscape with some local flavour, thus adding to the interest of the picture.

Robert R. Whale
View of Hamilton (1853),
oil on canvas, 90.6 × 120.8 cm.
Purchase, 1949.
Accession No. 4950.

Cornelius Krieghoff

1815–1872

A review of Cornelius Krieghoff's substantial *oeuvre* may at first leave us a little disappointed. That he was capable of fine and original work is evident from so many landscape and genre paintings, but along with these are many pictures of uneven quality and repetitious content. Such a situation—which presents many difficult problems of attribution—was not uncommon for nineteenth-century artists when facing the realities of making a living from their art in Europe and North America. Into his mid-forties Krieghoff was energetic, ambitious, prolific, and never short of schemes to further his interests. The range in his work was typical of many artists of his time, satisfying the demand for copies of well-known works of past and contemporary masters, as well as making copies and versions of his own compositions that had become popular. Krieghoff's success, as one of a relatively small number of professional artists in Canada, lay in defining his market: developing original compositions for a few collectors, and making copies and versions, particularly of his *habitant* and Indian subjects, as relatively inexpensive "souvenir" pieces.

We know little about Krieghoff's life before he and his brother arrived in New York around 1835. He was born in Amsterdam of a German father and Flemish mother but grew up in Germany, for the most part in Düsseldorf. He enlisted in the United States Army and spent three years in Florida during the Seminole Wars. He was discharged in 1840 and re-enlisted the same day for a further five years as a topographical artist. He received three months' advance pay. That, however, was the last the army saw of Krieghoff. It seems that he went immediately to Buffalo, where he met his brother, who had also absconded from military service, and the two crossed into Canada and settled in Toronto.

Krieghoff stayed in Toronto until 1845, apart from a year spent in Europe, and then moved to Montreal. It was there that he developed his reputation as a painter, as well as being noted as a man of culture and a celebrated conversationalist. He began to paint his *habitant* subjects based on the people among whom he lived in Longueuil, near Montreal. These charming, often humorous pictures of a harsh rural life were Canadian in their particulars but were based on the European tradition of genre painting. Their origins go back to the peasant themes of Pieter Brueghel the Elder and to seventeenth-century Dutch painters such as Adrian van Ostade, Jan Steen, and the Flemish painter Adrian Brouwer. Dutch genre and landscape painting enjoyed a revival in the earlier nineteenth century, with Düsseldorf as one of its principal centres; Krieghoff transposed this popular European fashion for his Canadian audience.

In 1853 John Budden, a Quebec auctioneer, friend and patron of Krieghoff, persuaded him to move to Quebec, promising to act as his agent in a city where he felt there was a good market for his work. There was almost no interest among the French in Krieghoff's paintings, but he found an enthusiastic audience in the prosperous English classes and the officers from the garrison. Krieghoff responded by broadening the range of his subjects, catering to the special interests of huntsmen and horsemen while continuing his *habitant* and Indian subjects. In the mid-1850s he made the first of his "bilking the toll" pictures, a subject which proved so popular that he fulfilled many orders for versions and copies. The new Indian compositions he developed in Quebec shifted the emphasis away from viewing the native people as curiosities towards showing them in the context of their traditional way of life.

Cornelius Krieghoff
Owl's Head and Skinner's Cove, Lake Memphremagog (1859),
oil on canvas, 43.3 × 63.8 cm.
Vincent Massey Bequest, 1968.
Purchase, 1968.
Accession No. 15490.

Cornelius Krieghoff
Merrymaking (1860),
oil on canvas, 88.9 × 121.9 cm.
The Beaverbrook Canadian Foundation. The Beaverbrook Art
Gallery, Fredericton.

Krieghoff's years in Quebec were not only the height of his success but were also the time when he produced his finest work. In genre painting his master-piece is *Merrymaking* of 1860 (Beaverbrook Art Gallery), which is based on the well-known Gendron Inn near Montmorency Falls and follows directly in the tradition of Pieter Brueghel and Jan Steen. Among the landscapes there are many fine examples, but none greater than the National Gallery painting of 1859, *Owl's Head and Skinner's Cove, Lake Memphremagog*. In this picture, Krieghoff brilliantly combined a dramatic vision with tightly observed detail. His attention to detail drew the praise of his contemporaries: "All his autumnal pieces . . .," the *Quebec Telegraph* recorded in 1862, "are remarkable for fidelity which rivals the photograph and cannot be surpassed."*

More striking to us perhaps are the Romantic over-tones of the picture: the swift changes from shadowy gloom to brilliant sunshine; the impression of great scale, though the picture is only some sixty-three centi-metres wide. Above all, there is the sense of nature's majestic indifference to human life which Krieghoff shows in the struggle of the two men in the rowboat.

Krieghoff's work declined suddenly in quality and quantity after 1862, possibly because of illness and family problems. In 1863 he assigned all his property to an A. J. Maxham, giving him power to settle his financial affairs, and then went to Europe. In the later 1860s, Krieghoff may have been living with his daughter in Chicago. He returned once to Quebec, in 1870; but although he was well received, he could not recapture the spark of his earlier days in a city whose character had changed substantially with the withdrawal of the British garrison in 1871. At the end of 1871, Krieghoff went back to Chicago, and he died there in March 1872 at the age of fifty-six.

*J. Russell Harper, *Painting in Canada: A History*, 2nd ed. (Toronto: University of Toronto Press, 1977), p.102.

Théophile Hamel

1817–1870

Théophile Hamel was the youngest of the three painters whose quality and creative innovation assured Quebec of its artistic pre-eminence in the fifty years between 1820 and 1870. He was apprenticed to Antoine Plamondon at the age of sixteen, just when Plamondon was beginning to assert his dominant position over the visual arts in Quebec. The fact that Hamel not only survived his lengthy training with Plamondon but flourished because of it would seem to be evidence of the young man's sanguine or complaisant disposition. It is all the more remarkable that Plamondon, given his jealous nature and his often unscrupulous treatment of competitors, seemed content to withdraw from the scene in the 1850s, at the time when Hamel was ready to come into his own.

Plamondon understood how important it was for a young artist to have direct knowledge of the great European masters, and he seems to have encouraged Hamel to travel. Hamel was abroad for three years, spending most of his time in Italy and supporting himself partly by making copies of masterpieces for Quebec clients. For his final year he went north, staying in Paris and Antwerp, where the ebullient paintings of Rubens made a particular impression on him. He returned to Canada in 1846.

The greater part of Hamel's career was devoted to fulfilling portrait commissions for prominent clergy and politicians. The institutional character of this work tended to mean restrained and conventional painting. Yet Hamel was capable of searching characterization, as is shown by paintings such as the 1853 portrait of *Mme. Marc-Pascal de Sales Laterrière* (Archbishop's Palace, Chicoutimi), whom he represented with a wistful but mature sentiment.

In many ways, at least to modern eyes, his most interesting works are his self-portraits. The earliest was done around 1837 when he was twenty. As if to show the range of his skills, he has set himself in front of a landscape that owes its form and atmosphere to Italian Renaissance models. The portrait itself is a little tentative, and his description of the body suffers from a limp bonelessness. It is a very different Hamel that we see in the *Self-Portrait* in the Musée du Québec, done five years later. Here, the artist stands among examples of his work, palette in hand, brush at the ready, as if he has been interrupted by our entrance into his studio. He turns confidently towards us, holding our gaze with eyes set deep beneath prominent brows, his features firmly defined by their enclosure with his mutton-chop whiskers. It is the image of the young artist ready to take on the world.

Fifteen years later, at the height of his popularity, Hamel painted companion portraits of himself and his wife. The figures are set against simple, plain backgrounds, modulated to give relief to the heads, which bear a clear, searching light. While the portrait of Madame Hamel is sympathetic and charming, the artist's view of himself is that of an anxious and rather weary man—a marked contrast to the dynamic of the Musée du Québec portrait. The turn of his head, angled slightly back, seems to seek support; and his eyes, rather than projecting their gaze towards us, seem to narrow and recede. Hamel was forty when he made this picture. He was at the top of his profession, sought after by the wealthy and influential from Toronto to Quebec. Yet, to himself, he could not deny a sense of resignation, even of disappointment.

Théophile Hamel
Self-Portrait (1842),
oil on canvas, 53.5 × 41.6 cm.
Musée du Québec.

Théophile Hamel
Madame Théophile Hamel (*c.* 1857),
oil on canvas, 76.6 × 60.8 cm; oval image on rectangular canvas.
Purchase, 1945.
Accession No. 4606.

Théophile Hamel
Self-Portrait (*c.*1857),
oil on canvas, 76.6 × 60.8 cm; oval image on rectangular canvas.
Purchase, 1945.
Accession No. 4605.

William Raphael

1833–1914

With the active careers of Krieghoff and Hamel on the decline in the early 1860s, Quebec relinquished to Montreal its position as the leading centre of artistic activity in Canada. Prosperity in Montreal was accompanied by a growing interest in the arts. The Art Association of Montreal was founded in 1860 and quickly became the most important art institution in the country. The prospect of patronage drew artists to the city, among the most important of whom were three German artists: Otto Jacobi, William Raphael, and Adolphe Vogt. They belonged to that numerous group of journeymen artists who travelled around Europe and North America in the mid- and late nineteenth century in search of work. Raphael was the only one of the three to make Montreal his permanent home: Jacobi was in the city in the 1860s and then divided his time among Montreal, Toronto, and Philadelphia; Vogt, who died before he was thirty, spent the last years of the decade in Montreal before moving to New York.

Raphael was born in Prussia and studied at the Royal Academy in Berlin. He was in New York in 1856, visited Montreal the following year, and returned to settle there around 1860. He became a solid member of the art community, joining the Society of Canadian Artists in 1867 and being elected to the Ontario Society of Artists in 1879 (part of Lucius O'Brien's drive to make this Toronto-based society a national institution). The following year he became one of the founding academicians of the Royal Canadian Academy.

Raphael was a good, if conventional, painter—a sound technician who on occasion produced some fine pictures. One such is the night scene, *Indian Encampment on the Lower St. Lawrence* (National Gallery), a virtuoso performance in its play of contrasting light sources—the moon, the beacon in the middle distance, and the campfire in the foreground. The painting was among those Raphael showed at the first RCA exhibition and the one he deposited as his diploma work. It was thus among the first pictures to enter the National Gallery collection.

The strength of the traditions of portrait and landscape painting in mid-century Canada allowed only a limited place for genre painting. "Low-life" genre pictures, based on seventeenth-century Dutch precedents, enjoyed a vogue in nineteenth-century Germany.

Krieghoff introduced the type to Canada, adapting it to local conditions, and Raphael made some pictures of this type. The area of the Bonsecours Market in Montreal seems to have held a special attraction for him. He was sketching there as early as 1857, and he made several paintings set in and around the market. Of these, *Behind Bonsecours Market, Montreal* of 1866 is unquestionably the finest.

The painting is a striking combination of a cityscape and genre subject, in which Raphael's special abilities in painting different qualities of light are given full play. The sky, the boats on the river, and the distant view of Île Sainte-Hélène are rendered with brilliant openness, contrasting with the play of light and shadow across the buildings in the middle ground. Among the figure groups there is a fine balance, ranging from the deep shade on the boy in the foreground to the sharp highlights on the two children listening to the fiddler. The market is filled with a wide range of people; and as was the tradition of this form of genre painting, Raphael comes close to caricature in some of the "types" he represents.

The figures, going about their business, develop a number of sub-themes which criss-cross the picture. The pivotal figure is the woman in a bonnet who is turned away from us. Her attention is drawn by a man holding up a cockerel; the man looks suggestively over to her, ignoring the woman to his left who vainly reaches up for the bird. In the foreground, uninterested in the activity, a boy plays with a dog while his companion, a caged bird by his side, gazes dreamily into middle distance. And perhaps it is the artist himself who stands in the centre of the picture, his portfolio under his arm. What of the five-branched candlestick he carries? Maybe Raphael is humorously suggesting that if art will not earn him a living, he will have to sell his possessions.

William Raphael
Behind Bonsecours Market, Montreal (1866),
oil on canvas, 67.5 × 109.6 cm.
Purchase, 1957.
Accession No. 6673.

Frederick A. Verner

1836–1928

Frederick Verner lived to a prodigious age, produced a substantial body of work, and earned a respected place in the story of how landscape painting in Canada came to be an assertion of national identity. Verner enjoyed popular success, though he had neither the natural talent nor the expressive vision of Lucius O'Brien or John A. Fraser, and his lasting reputation would have been all the more modest but for one painting, *The Upper Ottawa*, which ranks among the best works of the period.

Verner's early interest in art appears to have been inspired by seeing the work of Paul Kane. In 1856 he went to London to study, but the most notable aspect of his six years abroad was his enlistment in a volunteer force which in 1860–61 joined Giuseppe Garibaldi in his campaign to bring about Italian unification. Back in Toronto, Verner followed Kane by specializing in paintings depicting Indian life. In 1873 he made a trip through northern Ontario, going as far west as Lake of the Woods. The somewhat dry and scrappy sketches he made on this trip became the basis of his paintings for years to come. Even before this journey, a reviewer for the *Canadian Illustrated News* had remarked sarcastically on Verner's opportunism: "He appears to have hit upon a very popular vein, and will doubtless make a good thing of this affair."* The works he showed at the Ontario Society of Artists in 1874, after his western journey, were harshly treated by reviewers. The *Canadian Monthly*'s reviewer, for example, felt that the documentary interest of the paintings could not make up for their aesthetic deficiencies. Verner, he said, was "unable to enter the poetry of the scenes he paints, or to transfer the sentiment to his canvas."

Verner's association with O'Brien from the early 1870s on gave an important boost both to his career and to the quality of his work. He proposed the motion to elect O'Brien vice-president of the Ontario Society of Artists, and in 1883 the two men held a joint exhibition at the Burlington Gallery in London, England. Responding to the atmospheric character of O'Brien's painting and finding the means of developing a convincing sense of space, Verner sought the elusive "sentiment" which the critic said he lacked. His direct involvement in the Canadian scene ended in 1880 when he moved to England, though he visited Canada from time to time and continued to send work back for exhibition. He submitted regularly to the Royal Academy in England and was represented there half a dozen times between 1881 and 1900.

It was at the Royal Academy of 1882 that *The Upper Ottawa* was first shown; it was sent to the 1884 Royal Canadian Academy exhibition. In contrast to the lukewarm or negative notices Verner had often received, this painting brought him great praise. The reviewer for the *Week* was spurred to compete in eloquence with Verner's visual poetry: "The sky laughs, the water responds in this mirror, and the reflections dance. The wind must be present, so it comes in a gently wheeling eddy, and kissing the water marks the spot. . . . This is nature not painting."

A hundred years later our words might be different, but we have to agree that this is a remarkable painting, unprecedented in Verner's earlier work and unequalled subsequently. Infused with a brilliant silvery light, and painted with a free and delicate touch, it transcends the more common, prosaic character of Verner's usual style. We are left to enjoy its quiet mood and, perhaps, to regret that it is the only one of its kind.

*The quotations are from Dennis Reid, *"Our Own Country Canada"* (Ottawa: National Gallery, 1979), pp.240, 244, and 138–39.

Frederick A. Verner
The Upper Ottawa (1882),
oil on canvas, 83.5 x 152.3 cm.
Purchase, 1958.
Accession No. 6985.

Allan Edson

1846–1888

"The mists of morning give the scene a dreariness and shiveriness which is not pleasant, though quite in keeping with the subject. Just so may the old mountain have looked ages before the foot of man had disturbed the silence of the 'forest primeval' in the dim dawn when ancient night and chaos lay a-dying."*

With this purple-tinged encomium, a reviewer for the Montreal *Gazette* introduced his readers to the painting that drew so much attention at the 1871 exhibition of the Society of Canadian Artists. The painting in question was entitled *Mount Orford, Morning*, the work of the twenty-four-year-old Allan Edson. Edson was perhaps the most talented Canadian painter of his generation—a superb technician and, in contrast to the majority of mid-century journeyman painters, an artist of genuine creative development.

Edson was born in Stanbridge Ridge in the Eastern Townships of Quebec. He moved with his family to Montreal around 1860—his parents were in the hotel business—and soon began work as a clerk. He was employed by A. J. Pell, a Montreal art dealer who showed the work of Otto Jacobi, John A. Fraser, and the American artist Robert Duncanson. This may have been Edson's introduction to art, and by the mid-1860s he seems to have been receiving instruction from Duncanson. He spent a year studying in England, and by 1867, when back in Montreal, he was listing his occupation as "artist." The following year, he was represented in the first exhibition of the Society of Canadian Artists.

Edson's early work showed the influence of Jacobi, but from the start it had an individual intensity and directness. *Mount Orford, Morning*, which was more than one and a half metres wide, was not only ambitious for a young painter but was unusually large for the time. The scene has a grandeur arising from Edson's brilliant observations of light and colour—the way the clouds are lifting from the mountain, the flash of early sunshine in the middle ground, the density of the forests, the contrasts of dark and light across the still surface of the lake. But more than that, the painting expresses the sense of the primitive landscape, one that man has touched only at its edges. We are observers of the natural rhythms of change: the tree stumps at the water's edge which signal the slow process of growth and decay; and, in contrast, the tall trunks standing above the bush in the middle ground which indicate the swifter and more violent changes of forest fires and regeneration. Almost overlooked is the rowboat drawn up on the shore, a reminder of our brief, superficial intrusion on these surroundings. That Edson was making a specific point is revealed by the fact that this landscape was not as untouched as his image implies. Photographs taken by William Notman in 1867 from viewpoints similar to Edson's show that between the water and the mountains there was a broad area of cleared land dotted with settlers' houses.

*Dennis Reid, "*Our Own Country Canada*" (Ottawa: National Gallery, 1979), p.122.

Allan Edson
Mount Orford, Morning (1870),
oil on canvas, 91.6 × 152.8 cm.
Purchase, 1917.
Accession No. 1398.

Through the 1870s, Edson made a series of fine paintings of forest interiors, principally in watercolour. They are marked by scrupulously rendered detail and by a brilliant sparkling light filtering through the trees. An oil painting of this type made around 1875, *Trout Stream in the Forest* (National Gallery), was the work he submitted as his diploma piece for the Royal Canadian Academy.

The records concerning Edson become obscure in the mid-1870s. With a growing family, he may have been hard hit by the economic depression of those years. His fortunes seem to have improved in the new decade, and with them the direction of his work changed. After a spell of teaching at the Art Association of Montreal, he moved to Paris in 1881. There he studied with Léon Pelouse, an artist who had been associated with the Barbizon School. Edson's painting shifted towards a greater density of colour and more painterly surfaces. This is evident in the fine large *Land-scape* of around 1887 which stands in strong contrast to his work of the 1870s. This style, however, did not gain the same attention as his earlier painting. This was no doubt partly because of the unfamiliar location and partly because of the unfamiliar style.

Edson just preceded the fashion for French painting which a younger generation of Canadian artists—Brymner, Reid, and Harris, among others—was soon to introduce. Sadly, he never had the opportunity to develop this new mode fully, and thus to reap the rewards of changing tastes and ideas. He returned to Canada in 1887 after six years away (apart from a brief stay in Montreal in 1885) and settled in Glen Sutton in the Eastern Townships. Early in 1888 he fell ill with pneumonia and he died in May. He was just forty-one years old.

Allan Edson
Landscape (c.1887),
oil on canvas, 183.3 × 114.8 cm.
Purchase, 1974.
Accession No. 18161.

Lucius R. O'Brien

1832–1899

On 6 March 1880, Governor General the Marquis of Lorne stood before a packed and glittering audience in the Clarendon Hotel in Ottawa and formally opened the first exhibition of the Royal Canadian Academy. Those with the marquis included Lucius O'Brien, first president of the Academy; and behind them, holding pride of place on the wall, was O'Brien's *Sunrise on the Saguenay*, his Academy diploma work and, by tradition, the first work to enter the National Gallery collection.

The evening was a proud moment for both the Marquis of Lorne and O'Brien, who had worked closely together on the formation of the Academy—the marquis giving official and private support; O'Brien skilfully and patiently steering a path through the confused and often bitter debates among artists concerning the structure and procedures of the institution. The result of their efforts was a national cultural body expressive of contemporary political developments.

O'Brien was in his late thirties before he gave most of his time to art. He was born at Shanty Bay on Lake Simcoe, the son of a retired British army officer who had connections to the Irish peerage. He attended Upper Canada College and then entered a Toronto architect's office, subsequently studying and practising as a civil engineer. In 1873 he joined the recently formed Ontario Society of Artists, and the following year he replaced John A. Fraser as vice-president, thereby making himself a lifelong enemy.* Recognized by his peers as one of the best artists of the day, O'Brien received support in the society as a good leader and organizer. Establishing art societies and setting stand-

*The president and treasurer of the OSA were elected from non-artists, while the vice-president and secretary (the working officers of the society) were chosen from among the artist members.

Lucius R. O'Brien
Sunrise on the Saguenay (1880),
oil on canvas, 90.0 × 127.0 cm.
Royal Canadian Academy of Arts diploma work,
deposited by the artist, Toronto, 1880.
Accession No. 113.

The Glacier of the Selkirks
L. R. O'Brien
1886

40

ards for professional practice did not imply radical shifts in artistic interests. O'Brien was essentially conservative in his approach, and his values were based on ensuring that art in Canada gained a respected place within the mainstream of contemporary European and American art. The special character of art in Canada would arise from there being artists of high quality to respond to the range and character of the land.

O'Brien's own style was formed in the naturalistic mould typical of the mid-nineteenth century. Specifically, he was impressed by the Hudson River School painters in the United States, who had adapted European styles to their own land. While it is difficult to be convinced that he followed the more advanced "luminism" developed by some of the Hudson River artists, he does seem to have been influenced by the epic landscapes of Albert Bierstadt. Bierstadt was something of a favourite of both Lord Dufferin and the Marquis of Lorne, accompanying them on visits and staying at Rideau Hall—intimacies which no doubt impressed O'Brien.

Sunrise on the Saguenay responds to the evocative, lyrical side of the Hudson River School; the origins of the style reach back to the seventeenth-century French painter, Claude Lorrain. The paintings Lorrain made with early or late sunlight flooding directly towards the spectator were a special aspect of his work. O'Brien has used this effect here, finely controlling the complex, delicate mixtures of colour which describe the misty atmosphere of early morning. This he combines with an exaggerated scale of the cliffs in the manner of Bierstadt's majestic and poetic wilderness paintings.

It is interesting, however, that in the later 1880s, when O'Brien went west on the Canadian Pacific Railway to work in the Rockies, he did not indulge in the epic visions of the American West that mark the paintings of Bierstadt. O'Brien was deeply impressed by the mountain scenery, but his approach was to allow the landscape to determine his response rather than using it as the incentive for a Romantic interpretation filled with the extravagant devices of the sublime.

Lucius R. O'Brien
The Glacier of the Selkirks (1886),
watercolour over graphite on wove paper, mounted on wove paper, stretched on linen, 93.5 × 73.0 cm.
Purchase, 1982.
Accession No. 28056.

John A. Fraser

1838–1898

Through the 1870s and 1880s, Lucius O'Brien's leadership of the national artistic enterprise was dogged by a rivalry with John A. Fraser. The two men were a contrast in types: O'Brien, urbane Upper Canada aristocracy, looked up to as a leader; Fraser, son of a Chartist tailor, feisty, ambitious, and quick to take offence. Fraser received his early training at the Royal Academy schools in London. Immigrating to Canada in 1858, he joined William Notman's photographic studio in Montreal in 1860 and became its art director four years later. He moved to Toronto in 1868 to establish the Notman-Fraser studio, which he ran until dissolving the partnership in 1883.

Fraser's business responsibilities took up so much of his time that there were periods when he did little or no painting, but he always remained a presence on the art scene. His most important organizational initiative—which led to his first clash with O'Brien—came in 1872 with his forming the Ontario Society of Artists and becoming its first vice-president. Fraser offered the Notman-Fraser gallery for the society's first exhibition, held in 1873. Fraser showed six paintings on this occasion, including *September Afternoon, Eastern Townships* and *A Shot in the Dawn, Lake Scugog*, both of which are in the National Gallery collection. Later in 1873, Fraser's handling of some society matters and his autocratic leadership drew criticism from the membership. The society was divided on the issue, with O'Brien leading the majority opposition. In the result, O'Brien was elected vice-president and Fraser withdrew from the society he had founded, remaining outside until 1877.

Determined to make a significant showing at the inaugural exhibition of the Ontario Society of Artists, Fraser had no doubt worked very hard on the six paintings he exhibited. Dennis Reid has described how Fraser's development of spatial structure and his attention to detail reflected his knowledge of photography. Traditionally, space in landscape painting was structured on the basis of the spectator imaginatively taking a winding route into the countryside. With *A Shot in the Dawn, Lake Scugog*, space is built by disjunctive parallel planes, like the foreshortening effects of a camera. What does not belong to contemporary photography is the vivid colouring. A reviewer at the time credited this to Fraser's perception of the "clearness of our Canadian climate." Reid comments that it probably has more to do with the fashionable influence of the Pre-Raphaelites.*

In 1886, Fraser was praised by a professor at the Royal Academy in London for having "gone forth into the outer wilderness in search of the picturesque" in making some watercolours of the Rockies. In fact, Fraser did not leave his studio, for the pictures were based on photographs taken by Alexander Henderson. Subsequently, Fraser did make the trip west on the Canadian Pacific Railway and spent the summer and early fall of 1886 working in the mountains. The *Yale, B.C.* watercolour was among the works that arose from this trip. When the paintings were shown in Toronto later that year, they encouraged a *Globe* reporter to note that Fraser had risen to the mountains' "sublime plane and depicted their dizzy heights."**

These works represented Fraser's last rivalry with O'Brien, who also painted in the Rockies that year. They also mark the end of Fraser's direct commitment to art in Canada, for although he continued to exhibit at the Royal Canadian Academy in the 1890s, he was by that time directing the fortunes of his career to achieving success in New York and London.

*Dennis Reid, "*Our Own Country Canada*" (Ottawa: National Gallery, 1979), pp.216, 218.
**Ibid.*, p.393.

John A. Fraser
A Shot in the Dawn, Lake Scugog (1873),
oil on canvas, 40.6 × 76.4 cm.
Purchase, 1958.
Accession No. 6938.

John A. Fraser
Yale, B.C. (1886),
watercolour over graphite on wove paper, 45.8 × 66.1 cm.
Purchase, 1964.
Accession No. 14577.

William G. R. Hind

1833–1889

William Hind is an intriguing figure, attracting our attention while frustrating our desire to know more. There is perhaps an element of poetic justice in the fact that the elusive character of his art is matched by the scant information we have about him as a person. Hind seems to have enjoyed little in the way of an artistic reputation during his lifetime, and although a considerable amount of work survives, it was only in 1967, nearly eighty years after his death, that the first major exhibition of his work was organized. Hind's career coincided with the burgeoning development of artists' associations in Canada—associations which, in establishing professional standards, valued conformity; there was no easy place for Hind's individualism. When he died in Sussex, New Brunswick, in 1889, the local newspaper published an obituary which, in its shattering inadequacy, appears a perfect fit to contemporary opinions of the man. Hind, it was said, was "well informed, a good talker while inclined to be uncommunicative, fond of sports, and with a tendency to artistic matters; he had many friends by his grand and occasionally eccentric habits."*

*J. Russell Harper, *Painting in Canada: A History*, 2nd ed. (Toronto: University of Toronto Press, 1977), p.128.

William Hind was born in Nottingham, England, and came to Canada in 1851 at the age of eighteen, joining his brother Henry, a geologist and explorer, who had arrived a few years earlier. We know nothing of William's training, but he taught drawing at the Toronto Normal School from 1851 to 1857. He then returned to England, but was back in Canada in time to join Henry's 1861 expedition to Labrador as its official artist. The following year he set out on further travels, this time joining the "Overlanders of '62," a group who trekked westward to seek their fortunes in the goldfields of the Cariboo of British Columbia. Hind made an extensive pictorial record of the journey and of the lives of the gold miners. He then continued on to Victoria, which became his base for the next seven or eight years. He was some months in Winnipeg in 1870 and then moved to New Brunswick. He found work, possibly as a draughtsman, with the Intercolonial Railway and remained in the Maritimes the rest of his life, spending his last years in Sussex, New Brunswick.

William G. R. Hind
New Brunswick Landscape (*c.*1879–89),
watercolour and gouache with gum arabic on wove paper,
25.0 × 35.0 cm.
Transferred from the National Museums of Canada Trust
Collection, 1989.
Accession No. 30195.

Russell Harper, who was responsible for reviving interest in Hind's work, recognized in him the influence of the English Pre-Raphaelites.** Whether Hind saw paintings of these artists while in England or knew their work by reproduction is not clear, but his paintings do show the scrupulous attention to detail and the brilliant colour that characterize the Brotherhood's painting. More intriguing is how we may understand the sense of heightened intensity that characterizes Hind's work and transforms it from simple reportage into imaginative interpretation. There is a mysterious, unsettling aura about his work, and it has a naive quality, though only superficially. A glance at his *Self-Portrait* of around 1863 (McCord Museum, Montreal) reveals an image of self-scrutiny that is as artful as it is honest.

**J. Russell Harper, *William G. R. Hind (1833–1888)* [sic], *A Confederation Painter in Canada* (Windsor: Willistead Art Gallery, 1967).

The *New Brunswick Landscape* is a very recent acquisition for the National Gallery and likely dates from the last years of Hind's life. Although just a small watercolour, it gives us an extraordinary vision of the fall landscape. There is a vividness in its colour and an intensity of perception that sets it apart from the painting of those legions of artists who fulfilled the conventions of late-nineteenth-century landscape painting.

William G. R. Hind
Self-Portrait (c.1863),
watercolour, 30.5 x 22.9 cm.
McCord Museum of Canadian History, Montreal.

William Brymner

1855–1925

From the late 1870s, Paris was an irresistible magnet for a growing number of young Canadian and American artists. They found themselves in a vibrant city, at the heart of the most vital and complex art scene of the day. Our view of that situation has tended to focus most sharply on the conflict between the progressive inventions of Impressionism and the dead hand of the Academy, a conflict in which most North American artists took the conventional rather than radical course. The reality of the scene, however, was not so simply reductive; the desire for an art that was relevant to its time could be answered in many voices.

William Brymner was one of the first Canadians to join the stream of young artists going to Paris. His influence on succeeding generations of Canadian artists—and hence the influence of French art in Canada—was substantial, both because of the example of his work and because of the thirty-five years he taught at the Art Association of Montreal. His initial interest had been in architecture. He studied in Ottawa and then went to Paris in 1876 to continue his training. However, he soon turned to painting. Entrance for foreigners to the state-run École des Beaux-Arts was difficult, so Brymner enrolled at the Académie Julian, a private school that catered to foreign students. Masters from the Beaux-Arts came to the school each week to give critiques, but in general the students received limited formal instruction. Brymner was impressed by the major academic artists—Gérôme, Bouguereau, Bonnat, Meissonier—and also by the naturalistic style in modern-life subjects that was being made fashionable by younger contemporaries such as Bastien-Lepage and Dagnan-Bouveret.

William Brymner
A Wreath of Flowers (1884),
oil on canvas, 122.5 × 142.7 cm.
Royal Canadian Academy of Arts diploma work,
deposited by the artist, Ottawa, 1886.
Accession No. 19.

William Brymner
Early Moonrise in September (1899),
oil on canvas, 74.2 × 102.1 cm.
Purchase, 1908
Accession No. 42.

A Wreath of Flowers was painted in Paris in 1884. Brymner sent it back to Ottawa in 1886. That same year he returned to Canada and was elected to the Royal Canadian Academy, where the picture was presented as his diploma work and deposited at the National Gallery. In subject and style it is a typically French picture of its time. Ambitious and accomplished for an artist of twenty-nine, it marks Brymner neither as a radical nor as a reactionary, but no less as a painter of his times. The rural theme, the gentle charm of children playing on a summer's day, the precisely observed details, the soft atmosphere and light tones, set the painting firmly in its context. It is typical also in going further than a simple genre scene. Brymner's father, who took a close interest in his work, advised him to introduce "a story interest" in his paintings. He suggested subjects from Tennyson, mentioning in particular "Dora," a poem of family conflict and ultimate reconciliation centred on a child. The poem includes these lines:

> But when the morrow came, she rose and took
> The child once more, and sat upon the mound;
> And made a little wreath of all the flowers
> That grew about....

If Brymner did not illustrate this poem, he did respond to the belief that major painting meant reaching beyond mere visual description. Daisies have long been symbols of deceit, and although wreaths of flowers are made in the innocent play of children, they are also a reference to death. Here, the children sit on the hillside above the houses of the little coastal village where they live. Their freedom poignantly detaches them from the reality that they must eventually take on the cares of adulthood. Brymner expresses this by the picture's curious composition. The hillside cuts across the surface in a steep diagonal, and all the figures are set in the upper half. Equilibrium is established only if we project ourselves into the picture, as if we ourselves are climbing up the hill in counterpoise to the girl who is running down towards the seated group. We become engaged in the activity of the picture, objectively judging it as adults while subjectively completing it through our memories of childhood.

Paul Peel

1860–1892

There is little question that in the century since Paul Peel's death, his paintings have sustained their public appeal. However, their critical reception has been less constant. Peel's reputation became tarnished for two very different reasons. During the 1920s and 1930s, with the growing influence of the Group of Seven, his internationalism told against him. Unlike George Reid (who turned his American and French training to Canadian subjects and was viewed as something of a hero to nationalist interests), Peel became an expatriate and developed his subjects for an international audience. At a later stage, he was criticized for adhering to an academic style and to sentimental subjects when Impressionism was in full swing all around him. In recent years, Peel has been accorded a more positive reception. This is largely because of the scholarly attention now being paid to nineteenth-century academic art in an effort to redress the imbalance of an art history which for so long favoured an ''evolutionary'' sense of development.

Peel was something of a prodigy. He received his early drawing lessons from his father, a stone carver who had emigrated from England and settled in London, Ontario, where he helped found the Western School of Art and Design. At seventeen, in the face of stiff competition, Peel was accepted into the Pennsylvania Academy of Fine Arts, where he studied with Thomas Eakins. After three years there, he travelled to Europe and in May 1881 was in Pont-Aven in Brittany, already a popular artists' colony. The following year he entered the atelier of Jean-Léon Gérôme at the École des Beaux-Arts. Subsequently, he studied with Benjamin Constant, first at his atelier and then at the Académie Julian, when Constant was appointed a professor there.

There were a number of young Canadian artists studying and working in Paris at that time, but Peel was the one who received most attention. He had his first work accepted for the Paris Salon in 1883. In 1889 he had two major paintings accepted, *The Modest Model* (Columbus Museum of Art, Columbus, Ohio) and *A Venetian Bather*. The following year, two more were accepted: *Self-Portrait* (London Regional Art Gallery) and the work that was to bring him the greatest attention, *After the Bath* (Art Gallery of Ontario).

His work, particularly the latter picture, received warm praise from French and American writers, both for the charm of the themes and for the convincing technique. Peel returned home in 1890 and held an exhibition in London and subsequently an auction in Toronto. Although the notices were good, sale prices were disappointing. *A Venetian Bather* reached the highest price of $325. Sold to William Wakefield, it was lent to a Yonge Street bar room until the National Gallery purchased it five years later. It was perhaps the first painting of a nude to be publicly exhibited in Toronto. Peel went back to Paris but died there suddenly in October 1892. He was just short of his thirty-second birthday.

A Venetian Bather combines a number of references from the past. The title relates it to the tradition of Venetian painting and to the eighteenth-century fashion of pictures of ''la toilette,'' while the mirror evokes the iconographic overtones of *vanitas* and *veritas*, the indulgence of vanity and the revealing of truth. In this way, Peel brings the picture into the grand tradition. But in truth—and this probably accounted for a great deal of its contemporary appeal—the painting is really a genre picture; that is, its appeal lies not in the recapturing of a tradition so much as in the realistic presentation of an everyday scene. More than this, Peel has successfully added a degree of sentimental charm. The traditional subject of the bather and ''la toilette'' was concerned with adult figures; Peel's model is a young girl, and his emphasis is on the ambiguity between this child's potential of adulthood—with her as yet undeveloped sensuousness—and the fact that she is still attracted by the innocent play of a child, exemplified here by a kitten.

Paul Peel
A Venetian Bather (1889),
oil on canvas, 159.0 × 115.2 cm.
Purchase, 1895.
Accession No. 17.

Robert Harris

1849–1919

We owe to Robert Harris, more than to any other artist of his generation, our image of the people who formed and led Canada in the decades around the turn of the nineteenth and twentieth centuries. Tragically, his most important painting—the largest one and the one with the greatest historical significance—was lost. In 1883, recently returned from study in Paris, Harris was commissioned by the Government of Canada to paint *The Fathers of Confederation*. This involved thirty-four individual portraits, and Harris worked on it for nearly two years. The painting was destroyed in the great fire of 1916 that swept through the Parliament Buildings. We know it now through Harris's cartoon and preliminary sketches, and from contemporary copies and engrav-

Above: Robert Harris
A Meeting of the School Trustees (1885),
oil on canvas, 102.2 × 126.5 cm.
National Gallery of Canada

Below: Robert Harris
Preliminary Drawing for Fathers of Confederation (1883).
Confederation Centre of the Arts, Charlottetown.

ings. The commission established Harris's reputation and made him much sought after as a portraitist of the wealthy and influential.

Harris grew up in Charlottetown, Prince Edward Island, having emigrated with his family from Wales in 1856. His boyhood interest in art and his natural skills in drawing led him to seek professional training. He went first to Boston and then, in 1876, to the Slade School in London, England. The following year he moved on to Paris, where he studied in the studio of Léon Bonnat, one of the leading painters of historical subjects. Like William Brymner, who was also studying in Paris, Harris's training and his contacts in the Parisian art world kept him close to the academic mainstream. The stylistic orthodoxy of his work, coupled with the cachet of a Parisian training, brought Harris immediate attention when he returned to Canada in 1879. He settled in Toronto, and the following year he succeeded Lucius O'Brien as vice-president of the Ontario Society of Artists and became an academician in the newly formed Royal Canadian Academy. Then, in 1881, he went back to Paris for two years, studying again with Bonnat as well as at the Académie Julian. After completing *The Fathers of Confederation* in Ottawa early in 1885, he made Montreal his base, although he continued to travel frequently in Europe until shortly before his death in 1919.

Harris was a skilled portraitist in the conventional late-Victorian mode, as his paintings *Sir Hugh Allan* and *Sir Joseph Hickson* in the National Gallery demonstrate. More striking to our eyes perhaps are the searching late self-portraits (in the Agnes Etherington Art Centre and the Montreal Museum of Fine Arts) and the fine painting of his sister Sarah (in the New Brunswick Museum). In his own day, he was also well respected for his genre subjects: the National Gallery painting, *Meeting of the School Trustees*, 1885, struck a ready chord among contemporary audiences.

One of his finest pictures was neither a portrait in the proper sense nor a major narrative subject. It was the small and intimate *Harmony*. Made in 1886, this painting is of his wife Bessie playing the harmonium (she and Harris had been married the previous year). The painting is a sensitive evocation of its subject— Whistlerian in its development of painterly atmosphere. It is a finely tempered essay in the relationship between the discipline demanded in playing the instrument and the sounds emanating from it. Harris has captured the feeling of this by his balance between the precise drawing of the woman's head, torso, and hands, and the enveloping flow of light and shade around her.

Robert Harris
Harmony (1886),
oil on wood, 30.4 × 24.6 cm.
Purchase, 1957.
Accession No. 6757.

George A. Reid

1860–1947

The mid-nineteenth century saw a surge of interest in narrative painting. Pictures of this sort responded to the taste of the growing range and prosperity of the middle classes and reflected their values on educational, social, and moral issues. The subjects were chosen from historical or mythological themes and from contemporary themes. Artists tended to specialize in a particular approach.

In 1890, George Reid was thirty. He had returned to Toronto the previous November after a year in Paris and had immediately begun work on a large and ambitious canvas, *Mortgaging the Homestead*. He submitted the picture as his diploma work for the Royal Canadian Academy, to which he was elected as a full member in 1891. Reid's painting, recounting a country family's misfortune, struck a powerful chord in a society which was so dependent on the land. It was a subject Reid could invest with the conviction of personal experience. Born and brought up on a farm in western Ontario, he had had to overcome considerable resistance from his father to pursue his artistic interests. At one point, the family was forced to mortgage the farm. To such people, a mortgage was a last resort, a serious blow not only because it meant yielding independence and control of one's destiny, but also because it carried the shame and stigma of failure.

Ironically, what had been a low point in his family fortunes marked for Reid a major success in his career. Three years later, he painted in an even larger format a sequel, *Foreclosure of the Mortgage*. Widely exhibited across North America, this picture brought Reid highly favourable notices. (Regrettably, the painting was destroyed by fire in England in 1918. In 1935, Reid painted a second—and, one assumes, inferior—version from his original sketches, and this is now in the Government of Ontario collection.)

Mortgaging the Homestead was typical for its time because of its choice of theme and its narrative presentation. In the emphasis Reid put on the painting of light, he also showed himself responsive to the latest academic interests in Paris. The Salon of 1888, the year Reid went to Paris, was particularly noted for the emphasis that painters were giving to light effects. Yet unlike other Canadian artists who had gone to Paris (in particular William Brymner, Paul Peel, and Robert Harris), Reid did not fully adopt the French mode. Nor did his work indulge in the cloying sentimentality and heaping detail that characterized so much European painting of the time. His painting is spare in incident, concentrating on the strength of the characterization that he could bring to his figures.

The origin of Reid's approach owes most to the years he had spent in Philadelphia studying with Thomas Eakins, one of the finest figure painters of the day. Reid took up Eakins's robust naturalism and his concern with describing individuals rather than types. Eakins looked directly to the people and circumstances of his time and place, an attitude that also marks Reid's best work.

Reid invested a major commitment to the development of art in Canada through a long career as both painter and educator. When J. E. H. MacDonald wrote in the mid-1920s about the origins of an identifiably Canadian school of painting, he pointed to Reid as one of the most significant artists in its development. Reid taught from 1890 at the Central Ontario School of Art and Design, and he was president of the Ontario College of Art from 1912 to 1928. He became a great advocate of "public art" and undertook major mural decorative schemes at Toronto City Hall (1897–99) and the Royal Ontario Museum (1935–38). An extensive program of murals on historical themes at Queen's Park was not realized, but some of the subjects were later executed in murals at Jarvis Collegiate Institute in Toronto (1928–30). In 1944, shortly before his death, he donated to Ontario 459 paintings and works on paper, most of them for display and exhibition in schools across the province. Less than half of the works are traceable today.

George A. Reid
Mortgaging the Homestead (1890),
oil on canvas, 130.1 × 213.3 cm.
Royal Canadian Academy of Arts diploma work,
deposited by the artist, Toronto, 1890.
Accession No. 86.

Homer Watson

1855–1936

Homer Watson and the village of Doon are synony-mous. His work focused on the landscape around the southwestern Ontario community where he was born and to which he remained deeply attached. More than simply a record of the countryside, his paintings expressed the context of generations of people who had made their living from the land. In this respect, his representation of the landscape was a manifestation of the Canadian experience. "I have passed," he wrote, "the greatest part of my life in trying to paint the poetry, the easy joys, the hard daily work of rural life."* When, in 1907, Curtis Williamson and Edmund Morris founded the Canadian Art Club to encourage the best Canadian artists to live and work in Canada, they turned to Watson to become its first president.

Watson had little formal training, but two events at an early stage in his career brought him wide attention. He was included in the first Royal Canadian Academy exhibition in 1880 (thirty-eight years later he was to become the RCA's president); and his *The Pioneer Mill* was purchased by Princess Louise as a gift for her mother, Queen Victoria. Two years after this, Oscar Wilde, on his fiercely scheduled lecture tour of North America, saw a work of Watson's and pronounced him "the Canadian Constable." Curious though the comment was, Wilde followed through by later commis-sioning a work from Watson and helping him develop contacts in England.

The arch-sophisticate had selected for praise a man who had taken the decision to become an artist in desire and naivety. "I did not know enough to have Paris or Rome in mind," Watson wrote shortly before his death. "I felt Toronto had all I needed." What Toronto had was the country's first art museum, the Educational Museum of Upper Canada, opened in 1857. The museum collection, assembled by Egerton Ryerson, consisted mainly of copies of Old Master paintings and plaster casts of antique statues. It became Watson's "school." He also met John A. Fraser and may have received some informal instruction from him.

*Quotations are from J. Russell Harper, *Painting in Canada: A History*, 2nd ed. (Toronto: University of Toronto Press, 1977), pp.204, 202, and 208.

Homer Watson
The Flood Gate (*c.*1900–1901),
oil on canvas, mounted on plywood, 86.9 × 121.8 cm.
Purchase, 1925.
Accession No. 3343.

In 1876, Watson went to New York and met George Inness, one of the second generation of Hudson River School painters who was well acquainted with the Barbizon School and the work of Constable and Turner. Watson's early work reflects Hudson River School influence, though his lack of systematic training led to uneven results and often, in individual works, to clumsy passages. Beneath this, however, was a directness of vision which from time to time broke through in striking and haunting pictures, such as *Before the Storm* of 1887 (Mrs. G. Hudson Strickland) and *After the Rain*, 1883 (Beaverbrook Art Gallery).

Watson's early success broadened his ambition. He first went to England in 1887, and he returned there many times over the following decades. As he came in contact with original masterpieces, his work became more rigorous and disciplined; but in losing his naivety, he too often lost the sparkle of his best earlier work. Occasionally, however, he recaptured it, as in *The Flood Gate* of around 1900, painted when Watson was in his late forties. Watson looked on this as his masterpiece, deliberately choosing a subject that would bring

Homer Watson
After the Rain (1883),
oil on canvas, 81.3 × 125.1 cm.
Gift of Lord Beaverbrook.
The Beaverbrook Art Gallery, Fredericton.

comparison with Constable. The painting is not fluent in all respects. Placing the logs in the lower right to lead the spectator's attention into middle ground is a forced compositional device, and the huddled cattle are awkwardly scaled. Nevertheless, his depiction of the fury of the storm and the man's urgent attempt to release the pressure of the water is dramatically powerful. Add to this the fleeting effects of light in the sky and across the meadows, and the result is a painting of rare expressiveness.

Watson once wrote that "great artists are no more cosmopolitan than great writers, and no immortal work has been done which has not as one of its promptings for its creation a feeling its creator had of having roots in his native land and being a product of its soil." This was the essence of his own search, reached when the immediacy of his feelings broke through his restraint.

Maurice Cullen

1866–1934

Only in relatively recent years has broad attention been paid to the diversity of the Parisian scene in the 1880s and 1890s. The assumption of a contrast between the progressivism of the Impressionists and the conservatism of the Salon academics is, at best, simplistic. The fullness and complexity of the situation is reflected in the development of Canadian art history through the directions taken and the overlapping interests among Canadian painters who studied and worked in Paris. If Paul Peel and James Wilson Morrice represented the extremes between the academic and the progressive, William Brymner, George Reid, Maurice Cullen, and

others had distinct approaches, finding the measure of their interests within the range of art being made in Paris.

Maurice Cullen was born in St. John's, Newfoundland, but grew up in Montreal. His first artistic interest was sculpture, a rare choice in Canada, and he studied for three years with Louis-Philippe Hébert. He first went to Paris in 1889 and registered at the Académie Julian, where Peel and Reid were among the Canadians studying that year. Cullen soon turned from sculpture to painting and began working in the modified Impressionist style that was then popular, a style in which the

Maurice Cullen
Winter Evening, Quebec (c.1905),
oil on canvas, 76.2 × 101.9 cm.
Purchase, 1914.
Accession No. 1044.

Maurice Cullen
The Ice Harvest (*c.*1913),
oil on canvas, 76.3 × 102.4 cm.
Purchase, 1913.
Accession No. 740.

more traditional structure of landscape painting was given Impressionist surfaces and colour. He met Morrice, with whom he became good friends. He returned to Canada for the winter of 1895–96 and worked with Morrice in and around Quebec. Later in 1896 he returned to Europe and spent time again with Morrice in Venice. From the stay in Quebec, Cullen made *Logging in Winter, Beaupré* (Art Gallery of Hamilton), which was among the first Canadian "Impressionist" pictures. It is something of a hybrid in that it tries to transpose an approach developed for the colour and atmosphere of northern France and apply it to the Canadian landscape. Cullen deals impressionistically with the colour issues of light and shade on the snow, but the dark heavy trees are made on different painterly principles.

Cullen spent three years from 1897 in Montreal, but his work found little favour there. In 1900 he returned to Europe for two years, meeting up with William Brymner and Morrice. This two-year visit led Cullen further in the direction of loosening his approach and working in terms of an overall atmosphere. The results are seen in *Winter Evening, Quebec*, a very fine painting that he made around 1905. The real difference between this and his earlier work is that instead of thinking in the academic way of a scene comprised of discrete elements—trees, snow, sky, figures—he began here from the atmosphere of the whole scene. As a result, he has built a unified view that comes from seeing in terms of paint, freely forming the shapes of buildings, cliffs, and ice floes, and bringing sparkle to the scene by the brilliant spots of light which glow in the early dusk.

This freedom of painterly character continued through Cullen's work of the 1910s, such as the *The Ice Harvest* (*c*.1913), a painting made without dogmatic adherence either to academic structure or to Impressionist colour division. The progressive character of Cullen's work peaked at this time. From around 1920 he was living at Lac Tremblant in the Laurentians, and his painting gradually slipped into a more conservative approach—charming and finely painted landscapes, with which he enjoyed considerable success. However, his best work from the earlier years of the century had a significant influence on younger painters, most notably A. Y. Jackson, who attested to the impact that Cullen's painting had on him and on other members of the Group of Seven.

Maurice Cullen
Logging in Winter, Beaupré (*c*.1898),
oil on canvas, 63.9 × 79.9 cm.
Art Gallery of Hamilton.
Gift of the Women's Committee, 1956.

James Wilson Morrice

1865–1924

To many of his contemporaries, James Wilson Morrice epitomized the artist as outsider: the self-imposed exile from a country of which few of his acquaintances had any experience; the scion of a wealthy family who lived simply, though he dressed in hand-tailored English suits; a heavy and ultimately self-destructive drinker; an artist of genuine talent, whose work gained the respect of his peers in the intensely creative atmosphere of Paris at the turn of the century. He was the finest Canadian artist of his time—some would say of any time—and although he lived abroad most of his life, he maintained the hope, until finally discouraged in his later years, that Canada would show an openness to art long accepted everywhere else.

If remaining in Paris to make his career distinguished Morrice from his compatriots, so too did the fact that he involved himself directly in the advanced art of the day. And if, in 1911, he could say of the first Cubist works shown at the Salon d'Automne that he was incapable of understanding them, he had, for twenty years, responded to the complex changes in advanced art, from Impressionism to the Fauves, without yielding the distinction of his own touch and vision. He was a Post-Impressionist painter, not by the adoption of a style but by virtue of his own art.

Morrice was born in Montreal, one of eight children of a wealthy Scots Presbyterian family. His interest in art was apparent in childhood, but he studied to gain admission to the Ontario Bar. That done, he devoted his life to art, enjoying the freedom of a private income. He studied briefly at the Académie Julian and also with Henri Harpignies. He was quickly accepted into the artistic milieu in Paris, at first principally in the anglophone community but later enjoying the friendship of Henri Matisse, Albert Marquet, and other French artists. Still, his reputation was as something of a loner. Arnold Bennett described him in *Sketches for an Autobiography* as characterized by an elusive melancholy. Somerset Maugham, who modelled his hero Warren on Morrice in *The Magician* (1908), wrote: "The further he goes from sobriety the more charming he is. He's the only man in this room of whom you'll never hear a word of evil. The strange thing is that he's very nearly a great painter. He has the most fascinating sense of colour in the world."*

*G. Blair Laing, *Morrice: A Great Canadian Artist Rediscovered* (Toronto: McClelland and Stewart, 1984), p.110.

James Wilson Morrice
The Ferry, Quebec (1907),
oil on canvas, 62.0 × 81.7 cm.
Purchase, 1939.
Accession No. 4301.

James Wilson Morrice
A Street in the Suburbs of Havana (*c*.1915–21),
oil on canvas, 54.4 × 65.0 cm.
Gift of an anonymous donor, 1982.
Accession No. 28135.

Morrice's arrival in France in 1890 coincided with the opening of one of the most vital and surging quarter-centuries in western art. He was drawn by various possibilities—through Impressionism and then, encouraged by the American painter Robert Henri, to a re-evaluation of Édouard Manet, and finally to his own discovery of James McNeill Whistler, whose work had a profound effect on him. In these years he was still anxious to express his Canadian background and experience. Significant in this regard was his meeting with Maurice Cullen; the two men worked together in Quebec in the winter of 1895–96, and Morrice was influenced by the way Cullen sought to adapt Impressionism to the light and atmosphere of the Canadian winter. By the turn of the century, Morrice had established his own personal manner, one with a range that responded to his vision of the changing conditions in which he worked—from the atmosphere of northern France, to the Canadian winter, to the golden light and faded pastel colours of Venice.

Paintings by Morrice with Canadian subjects are relatively rare, and rarer still are those, like *The Ferry, Quebec*, which are substantial in size. The title of the picture refers to the ferry plying between Lévis and Quebec, but the picture's true subject is the grip of winter. Morrice worked the painting up from a small oil sketch. He held close to this preliminary sketch, making only a few changes, such as eliminating the quayside in the lower right and giving the house on the left more prominence in order to strengthen the composition.

Morrice's contemporary reputation was as a colorist, yet the fascination of his work—like that of Matisse—is in the play between colour and drawing. His painterly response is, in essentially abstract terms, first to the broad relationships of colour, and then, through drawing, to suggest specific forms within the colour masses. Look, for instance, at the way he defines the structures on the distant cliffs without describing them, and at the way he repeats a similar undulating black line in front of the house in the lower left. Look also at the way in which, without making any essential shift to the overall colour, he builds up the pierside building in the lower right. The feeling for winter exists in the colour— the grey blue of the water and the grey sky tinged with that curious pink hue of snow-laden stratus, an ironic warmth echoed in the dull red of the roof of the house. The painting is a brilliant evocation of a bone-chilling northern day.

Nothing is more telling of the character of Morrice's work than to turn from *The Ferry, Quebec* to *A Street in the Suburbs of Havana*. By his use of colour, cold is transformed to warmth, and the broad harmonies are given specific form by freely drawn linear elements. In his later work, Morrice drew encouragement from the work of the Fauves, who had first shown at the Salon d'Automne in 1905. He painted with Matisse in Tangier in 1912 and 1913, and his work shows a growing warmth and richness of colour, which matches the colours of North Africa to the freedom of colour that Fauvism had introduced. The work of his later years is concentrated on the lush, full settings of places in the sun: Cuba, North Africa, Jamaica, and Trinidad. But with this went a steady deterioration of his health as the effects of years of alcohol abuse gripped his body. His ability to work was seriously affected from 1921 on, and he died in the Military Hospital, Tunis, in January 1924.

Marc-Aurèle de Foy Suzor-Coté

1869–1937

In 1913, Edmond Dyonnet, secretary of the Royal Canadian Academy, asserted that "no French-Canadian painter fortunately has dreamed of following in their folly those despisers of art [i.e., the Impressionists] who have undertaken the mission of denying beauty and proscribing truth."* Whether Dyonnet was being deliberately obscure, or whether he was hoping that saying it was not so would make it not so, it is hard to tell. The fact is that since Marc-Aurèle de Foy Suzor-Coté had returned to Canada in 1907, he had been painting landscapes in a Late Impressionist manner. In this, Maurice Cullen and James Wilson Morrice had preceded him by more than a decade—and only in contrast to hidebound academicism could Suzor-Coté be described as radical; but he did adapt the lightness and openness of Impressionist texture to a particular aspect of the Canadian landscape.

Suzor-Coté was born in the village of Arthabaska in the Eastern Townships of Quebec. His introduction to art and his initial training, like that of Ozias Leduc and Paul-Émile Borduas, came from church decoration. In 1891 he went to Paris and studied at the École des Beaux-Arts under Léon Bonnat. On his second visit to Paris, 1897–1907, he took a broader view of the art around him. He enrolled at both the Académie Julian and the Académie Colarossi, and painted a wide range of subjects. The National Gallery's *The Art Lover* of 1899 is a fine if typical example of the genre painting of the day. Towards the end of his ten-year stay in France, Suzor-Coté began to adopt an Impressionist mode and to make the first works on the theme that he was to paint so often after his return to Canada, that of the river in winter. The popularity of this subject in the late nineteenth century was due in large part to the Norwegian, Fritz Thaulow. As was true for many Canadian painters, Thaulow sought to unite his respect for French art with the special qualities of his homeland.**

*J. Russell Harper, *Painting in Canada: A History*, 2nd ed. (Toronto: University of Toronto Press, 1977), p. 236.

**Jean-René Ostiguy, *Marc-Aurèle de Foy Suzor-Coté: Winter Landscape. Masterpieces in the National Gallery of Canada, No. 12* (Ottawa: National Gallery, 1978), p.6.

Marc-Aurèle de Foy Suzor-Coté
The Art Lover (1899),
oil on canvas, 82.0 × 95.5 cm.
Purchase, 1983.
Accession No. 28234.

Marc-Aurèle de Foy Suzor-Coté
Winter Landscape (1909),
oil on canvas, 72.2 × 94.4 cm.
Gift of Arthur S. Hardy, Ottawa, 1943.
Accession No. 4574.

It was in 1909 that Suzor-Coté made his first two Canadian winter scenes: *Settlement on the Hillside* and the *Winter Landscape*. Both are in the National Gallery collections. *Winter Landscape* was exhibited in Paris in 1911 and in St. Louis in 1918 (on the latter occasion, under the invigorating title *The Splendour of Our Canadian Winter*). The subject for both these paintings, as for most of his landscapes, was the countryside around Arthabaska. The village of Arthabaska is the settlement on the hillside, and the *Winter Landscape* is of the Nicolet River and Mont Saint-Michel, but in conflict with Impressionism's emphasis on *plein-air* painting, it is probably a compilation of several views rather than a direct record of the artist's experience.

In *Winter Landscape*, Suzor-Coté has made extensive use of the palette knife, creating a complex, pitted surface which scatters the light of the late afternoon sun. On the snowy river banks the paint is thickly built up, but for the river he has dragged the paint over the red-brown underpaint that serves as the reflections of the banks where the snow has melted. The structure of the painting is built up from a series of long, contiguous lines, which describe and unite the distant hills, the sloping river banks, the flow of the water. The emphasis on these sinuous lines may suggest the influence of the Art Nouveau style which was so pervasive around the turn of the century. This does not, however, imply a Symbolist reading for the painting. Suzor-Coté's approach was essentially a naturalistic response to the countryside he knew so well. If Impressionism, even in 1913, was an abomination of untruthfulness to Dyonnet, it had become for many artists, because of its sensitive interpretation of the effects of light and colour, a "natural" response to perceptual experience.

Suzor-Coté's artistic career was ended by a stroke in 1927. His landscape paintings stand as a significant contribution to the identity of the northern landscape as a reflection of rural rather than wilderness life. In contrast to the Group of Seven, who asserted the northern landscape as a nationalist metaphor, Suzor-Coté's view was of a landscape loved for its familiarity.

Ozias Leduc

1864–1955

There are several ways in which the work of Ozias Leduc may be said to be concealed. His most widely seen paintings were the large-scale decorative schemes he painted on the walls and ceilings of cathedrals, churches, and bishops' palaces across Quebec—some hundred and fifty paintings in twenty-seven locations. Leduc made his living by these commissions; but although they were open to public view and constituted the serious pursuit of a devout man, they were concealed behind the direction of those who had ordered them and behind the themes that Leduc had been given to illustrate.

By contrast, Leduc's easel pictures were the private expressions of a private man. In over sixty years of work, he held only one solo exhibition: at the Biblio-thèque Saint-Sulpice, Montreal, in 1916. Between 1891 and 1920 he did send paintings to the annual exhibitions of the Art Association of Montreal, the Royal Canadian Academy, and the Ontario Society of Artists, where they drew the admiration of a small but appreciative group of people. However, he stopped submitting to exhibitions after 1920, the period when much of his important church work was done.

There is a third sense in which Leduc's work is concealed. His easel paintings—the portraits of friends and the landscapes and genre scenes of rural Quebec, such as *Pommes vertes*—appear withdrawn from the debates which surrounded art in the late nineteenth and early twentieth centuries. They seem wholly invested in a mysticism of the everyday by their simplicity of subject, expressed in a gentle but direct style. On Leduc's one trip abroad (he accompanied Suzor-Coté to France in 1897), the art that impressed him most was that of some minor Impressionists, in particular Le Sidaner. However, at a later stage, friends who discerned the affinities between his interests and the broader contemporary scene in Europe encouraged him to read the work of Huysmans and Émile Mâle, and to look at the paintings of the Symbolists, even if only in magazines. Further, because of his work for the church, he took a close interest in the ideas and methods of Maurice Denis, whose Atelier d'Art Sacré was founded in 1921 to encourage modern artistic expression in doctrinaire religious painting.

Ozias Leduc
Pommes vertes (1914–15),
oil on canvas, 63.3 × 94.4 cm.
Purchase, 1915.
Accession No. 1154.

Ozias Leduc
L'Enfant au pain (1892–99),
oil on canvas, 50.7 × 55.7 cm.
Purchase, 1969.
Accession No. 15793.

Leduc worked on *L'Enfant au pain* over a period of seven years. Several people have found a parallel between the painting and the work of the eighteenth-century French master, Jean-Baptiste Chardin, whose simple and solid values are in such contrast to the mass of gilded, extravagant decoration that was characteristic of his time. For Leduc, the reference is probably less to Chardin himself than to the fact that they both belonged to the longer tradition of genre painting, which originated in seventeenth-century Holland and was continually reinvented through the centuries. Leduc's *L'Enfant au pain* is a painting of the Quebec of his day, just as Chardin's paintings responded to an aspect of French life in his day, and just as the earlier Dutch painters reflected their time.

The painting tells of rural Quebec life, the life that was Leduc's own. He represents its tough conditions—the boy's torn shirt, the plain furniture, the frugal meal, the simple instrument on which the boy plays—but draws from them a warmth and richness that transcends the modest circumstances of the scene. He does this through the sensitivity with which he gives and withholds emphasis. The bowl and spoon, the crust of bread, the corner of the table, the end of the mouth organ, and the boy's sleeve are all painted in sharp, light-rich focus. Elsewhere the focus is softer, the textures more absorbent, the light less reflective. At first sight, the balance seems curious; for, with our attention drawn to the highly lit, sharply focused areas, only slowly do we appreciate that the music making is the centre of the picture. The heart of the picture is concealed from us. In the final result, however, we realize that the truth Leduc expresses lies not in the objects that can be shown but in what cannot be shown—the depth of feeling that arises from the making of music, no matter how humble the surroundings.

Clarence Gagnon

1881–1942

For some seventy-five years after William Brymner went to Paris to study in 1876, the city was the chosen destination for young Canadian artists, especially those from Quebec. Individual artists sought the stimulus and challenge of Paris at a time when the sense of cultural life in Canada was growing stronger. The result was a complex relationship between their desire to be part of the larger scene and their interest in deepening and expanding the quality and quantity of the indigenous scene. Although there were exceptions—James Wilson Morrice and, to a lesser extent, Maurice Cullen—most Canadian artists going to Paris found their point of reference within the mainstream rather than in the progressive elements.

Clarence Gagnon was a student of Brymner at the Art Association of Montreal. Graduating in 1900, he began painting landscape and village subjects in the Baie-Saint-Paul region of the north shore of the St. Lawrence. With the support of a wealthy Montreal collector, James Morgan, he went to Paris in 1904 to study at the Académie Julian. Gagnon knew Morrice and admired his work, but rather than following the more radical directions that Morrice was taking, Gagnon was drawn to the popular conventional versions of Impressionism. When he returned to Montreal in 1909, he began to adapt these methods to his rural Quebec subjects. *The Wayside Cross, Autumn*, which he painted around 1916, shows clearly his way of linking a more traditional naturalism with the atmospheric effects and high-keyed colour of Impressionism. Lacking the formalism of Morrice, Gagnon's approach also remained distinct from Cullen's more thorough attempts to reconcile the structure of Impressionist painting with the particular character of the Canadian landscape.

Gagnon returned to Paris in 1917–19 and again in the mid-1920s. He remained there until 1936, gaining a significant reputation as an illustrator. He continued to paint Quebec subjects—the *Village in the Laurentians* of around 1924 (National Gallery) is one of the best known—but he moved away from his earlier Impressionist style and developed a colourful, decorative manner for his densely detailed pictures. His work stands in contrast to that of A. Y. Jackson, who in his almost annual trips to Quebec covered similar ground to Gagnon. Gagnon took exception to the influence that the Group of Seven wielded; he wrote in 1927 of the "Seven Wise Men" occupying the "Seven Rooms" of the "House of Seven" and excluding younger artists who thought differently from them. The radical and nationalist direction of the Group was to become a sort of academicism and a limiting factor on new developments. Gagnon's difference of opinion with the Group was a classic example of the tension between those who looked outside and those who turned inwards, but with the twist that the more radical position in this case was taken by those who turned their backs on the international scene.

Clarence Gagnon
The Wayside Cross, Autumn (*c.* 1916),
oil on canvas, 56.0 × 74.5 cm.
Purchase, 1916.
Accession No. 1367.

J. E. H. MacDonald

1873–1932

J. E. H. MacDonald was the oldest member of the Group of Seven and, with Lawren Harris, was responsible for its early development.* As a senior artist at the Toronto graphic design firm of Grip Ltd., he was a major encouragement to the younger painters working there. Later, he became the unofficial spokesman for the Group of Seven, responding publicly to the criticisms levelled against it. He was insistent in asserting a historical context for the Group's emergence and purpose, tracing the origins of a truly Canadian art movement to men such as George Reid, C. W. Jefferys, and William Cruickshank (with whom he studied) and to groups such as the Toronto Art Students' League and the Graphic Arts Club.

In 1911, MacDonald held an exhibition of his paintings at the Arts and Letters Club, to which he had recently been elected. Jefferys wrote of these paintings: "Mr. MacDonald's art is native—as native as the rocks, or the snow, or pine trees, or the lumber drives that are so largely his themes. . . . So deep and compelling has been the native inspiration that it has to a very great extent found through [MacDonald] a method of expression in paint as native and original as itself."** The exhibition made a profound impression on Lawren Harris, and he and MacDonald began to work together, forming the nucleus of the Group of Seven.

Their entries at the 1912 Ontario Society of Artists exhibition brought MacDonald and Harris considerable attention from the critics, who were aware that they were witnessing something new, even if it resisted definition. For MacDonald and Harris, that definition became clearer as a result of visiting the Albright Art Gallery in Buffalo to see a major touring exhibition of contemporary Scandinavian art. They had known of this type of work through magazines, but were struck at the exhibition by the strength of the artists' responses to the northern landscape. The Scandinavian painters, MacDonald said, "began with *nature* rather than with *art*" and their paintings seemed "true souvenirs of that mystic north around which we all revolve."†

MacDonald moved tentatively at first, his paintings still closer in character to the Parisian-influenced Suzor-Coté and Maurice Cullen. Nevertheless, he assumed the leadership in advocating the new direction. And when the fledgling group's 1913 exhibition at the Arts and Letters Club drew from H. F. Gadsby an article in the *Toronto Star* entitled "The Hot Mush School, or Peter and I," it was MacDonald who defended their approach. Three years later, he was to write again, this time in the Toronto *Globe*, in response to criticisms of the group's entries in the 1916 Ontario Society of Artists exhibition.

---

*The seven artists who founded the Group of Seven were J. E. H. MacDonald, Lawren S. Harris, Arthur Lismer, A. Y. Jackson, Frank H. Johnston, Franklin Carmichael, and F. H. Varley—but not Tom Thomson, for he was dead by the time the Group was officially formed.

**J. Russell Harper, *Painting in Canada: A History*, 2nd ed. (Toronto: University of Toronto Press, 1977), p. 271.

†Dennis Reid, *The Group of Seven* (Ottawa: National Gallery, 1970), p.33.

J. E. H. MacDonald
The Tangled Garden (1916),
oil on beaverboard, 121.4 × 152.4 cm.
Gift of W. M. Southam, F. N. Southam, and H.S. Southam,
1937, in memory of their brother Richard Southam.
Accession No. 4291.

J. E. H. MacDonald
The Solemn Land (1921),
oil on canvas, 122.5 × 153.5 cm.
Purchase, 1921.
Accession No. 1785.

He clashed in particular with Hector Charlesworth, who had selected MacDonald as "the chief offender . . . [throwing] his paint pots in the face of the public." MacDonald entitled his riposte "Bouquets from a Tangled Garden," a reference to his most important canvas in the exhibition.

Ironically, *The Tangled Garden* was not concerned with a "northern" subject; it was a painting of MacDonald's garden in Thornhill, just north of Toronto. In formal terms, the picture is conventionally structured. Three drooping sunflowers define the front plane, while a fourth is set back to establish depth; the central sunflower marks the mid-point of the picture's span and puts the spectator's eye level two-thirds of the way up from its lower edge. But this underpinning is concealed by the impact of bursting colour, which MacDonald has laid down forcefully, breaking free from the controlled, modified Impressionism of his earlier work. And all this is in a picture of ambitious scale. One of Charlesworth's specific criticisms of the painting was that it was too big for "the relative importance of the subject." In an inverted way, this went directly to the very strength and daring of the picture, for MacDonald showed that the painter did not need to start with a "scene"—that some small and unconsidered corner of nature could contain everything if one were prepared to grasp it.

The brilliance of colour and the dense surface of the painting, countered by the traditional formal structure, exemplify the tension in MacDonald's drive: the desire for a new expression arising from an essentially conservative image of nature. The core of this is most fully represented by his 1921 *The Solemn Land* of the Montreal River in Algoma. This painting was the high point in his search for a "true souvenir of that mystic north." Yet in its dour colouring and decorative drawing, it seems trapped between his response to the fullness of nature and its symbolic transcendence. By contrast, *The Tangled Garden*, for all its confusion between rigid structure and anarchic detail, has a rare freedom and joyousness.

Tom Thomson

1877–1917

There are a few works of art that so represent their time and place as to transcend the usual categories of description and criticism. Tom Thomson's *The Jack Pine* is such a work. Widely known by exhibition and reproduction, it has been for generations of Canadians the painting most closely identified with the image of their land. Its very familiarity, however, keeps it hidden in plain sight, set ambiguously between a shallow cliché and an icon of deep and indefinable power. And what of Thomson himself? A loner, at first diffident about his art, he was in his mid-thirties before he began to paint seriously. His abilities were then quickly recognized by his colleagues. His early death has encouraged the myth of the raw genius and the mystique of unfulfilled promise, concealing Thomson's real achievements. There is nothing raw about *The Jack Pine*. It is a precise and rationally constructed image, arising from Thomson's ability to retain the painterly freedom which marks his oil sketches from nature while transposing the rough sketch into a finely attuned, pictorial structure.

Thomson earned his living as a designer and illustrator. Around 1908 he went to work for the Toronto firm of Grip Ltd., where he met J. E. H. MacDonald and subsequently Arthur Lismer. MacDonald encouraged him to paint, but his true awakening came through an extended stay in Algonquin Park and the Mississauga Forest Reserve in the spring and summer of 1912. Thomson developed a routine of going to the park each year (from 1915 on, working as a guide and fire ranger) and making oil sketches, which he painted up during the winters in Toronto.

Thomson drew on the training and experience of the artists who would subsequently form the Group of Seven: first, MacDonald; then A. Y. Jackson, with whom he shared space in the Studio Building in 1914; Lismer the following year, during a trip they took to Algonquin Park; and Lawren Harris during the winter and spring of 1915–16. These artists recognized in Thomson a rare intuition of the relationship between his perception of the landscape and the character of painting. Lismer described how, "when the rest of us were slaving to harmonize the contrast of some autumn colour-composition, I have seen Tom leisurely open his sketch box and allowing himself to go with the stream catch in a few moments the spirit of the scene without being at any time conscious of our problems."[*] It was this directness—this freedom with which he absorbed the scene in front of him and gave it a painterly equivalent—that is the achievement of Thomson's small oil-on-board sketches such as *Autumn Foliage*.

[*] Dennis Reid, *Tom Thomson: The Jack Pine. Masterpieces in the National Gallery of Canada, No.5* (Ottawa: National Gallery, 1975), p.28.

Tom Thomson
Autumn Foliage (1916),
oil on wood, 26.7 x 21.5 cm.
Purchase, 1918.
Accession No. 1544.

Tom Thomson
Spring Ice (1916),
oil on canvas, 72.0 × 102.3 cm.
Purchase, 1916.
Accession No. 1195.

These sketches were made swiftly. The structure was shaped with a few broad areas of colour, and the surface was then layered over with short, thick strokes of pure colour to grasp the essential impressions of the scene. Little time was spent on tonal balance or detail. The curving areas of brown in the lower left and right of *Autumn Foliage* do not so much define the foreground space as delimit the area of peripheral vision and focus attention on the centre. The illusion of deep space, across the lake to the distant hills, is achieved by sharp colour contrasts. It is with a similar use of colour alone that Thomson describes how the sky arches over us, achieving this by arbitrary dashes of pink and purple. The impression of scale is given by the bare branches of the trees, which he set down last to articulate the broad regions of colour.

The instinctive grasp of painterly expression that Thomson showed in his oil sketches was not easily transferable into the larger compositions he made in the studio; he needed a structure within which to work. Along with other members of the Group, his approach was based on Art Nouveau design (his training had been in design rather than fine art). In one of his earlier major paintings, *Northern River* of 1914–15 (National Gallery),

that sense of design seems to overcome the immediacy of feeling for light and atmosphere. By 1916, in *Spring Ice*, although the composition remains rigidly ordered, it is the strength of colour that dominates. Then, in *The West Wind* (Art Gallery of Ontario) and *The Jack Pine*, the decorative character is more pronounced; the extraordinary strength of these paintings lies in how Thomson has brought the vitality of the sketches into powerful formal designs.

These two paintings were made immediately after Thomson had worked closely with Lawren Harris. Even at this early stage, Harris, more than any of the Group, was driving towards a rigorous formalist-coloristic structure. Thomson was surely influenced by this, particularly after the two men worked together in the northern part of Algonquin Park early in 1916. It was here that Thomson made the sketch for *The West Wind* and most probably also for *The Jack Pine*.

Thomson returned to Toronto in November, to the combined living quarters and studio in the renovated shack behind the Studio Building that he had occupied the previous year. Over the winter, he painted a group of major canvases, including *The Jack Pine*. He returned to Algonquin Park in March 1917 and settled into a routine of guiding and sketching, using Canoe Lake as his base. On 8 July, he set off for an overnight fishing trip. Later that day, his overturned canoe was spotted, but his body was not discovered until eight days later.

The Jack Pine was purchased by the National Gallery in the spring of 1918 when Eric Brown, director of the gallery, described it as the best picture of any kind that Thomson ever painted. Its almost square format gives a sense of calm and stability, which Thomson carries through in the geometry of the composition. While this underlying structure is probably sensed rather than seen, what is clearly visible on the surface of the painting is how the sky and the water are painted in broad horizontal bands. The gently curving forms of the earth impose into the unity of sky and water; and the soaring reach of the tree, extending even beyond the limits of the painting, is countered by the downward slope of the branches and the dense, heavy foliage.

Another element, too, is worthy of consideration. Theosophy played an important part in the thinking of many visual artists of the time, and it was to be significant for several of the Group of Seven painters, in particular Lawren Harris. There is little evidence about Thomson's knowledge of these ideas; still, to describe *The Jack Pine* wholly in naturalistic terms is to miss the point of a sophisticated and finely calculated painting. In this picture, as in *The West Wind*, Thomson was beginning to take a direction which, going beyond the purely decorative effects of Art Nouveau, transformed the immediate experience of nature into a symbolic structure of landscape. Through this, he was reaching beyond the particularities of time and place to an expression that was universal in its appeal.

Tom Thomson
The Jack Pine (1916–17),
oil on canvas, 127.9 x 139.8 cm.
Purchase, 1918.
Accession No. 1519.

Lawren S. Harris

1885–1970

Lawren Harris was a rare and powerful force in Canadian art. He was a force rather than simply an influence. His drive to action and his inspiration for others was linked to his artistic skills and to the demands he continually set on his own paintings as expressions of valid meaning. The potential of his stature remains unfulfilled, for more than half of his life's work—that painted after 1936—has yet to receive the full attention it deserves.

Looking back on the Group of Seven years, A. Y. Jackson wrote, "While we rather prided ourselves that the Group had no leader, without Harris there would have been no Group of Seven. He provided the stimulus; it was he who encouraged us always to take the bolder course, to find new trails."*

In 1911, then aged twenty-six and recently returned from studies in Berlin, Harris sought out J. E. H. MacDonald, whose landscape paintings had so impressed him, to form the nucleus of a group that would give expression to the "character, atmosphere, moods, and spirit of Canada." Harris's work quickly showed the influence of the Scandinavian art which he and MacDonald saw in Buffalo early in 1913. *Snow II*, which he painted in 1915, reflects his response to the work of the Swedish artist Gustaf Fjaestad,** but it also shows clearly Harris's firmness of painterly structure and his emphasis on the simplification of form over a density of detail.

Harris played a major role in persuading Jackson to join the Group in 1913. In the same year, he put up most of the money to build the Studio Building of Canadian Art, which was to be a centre for the Group of Seven's activities. However, the pace of their work was interrupted by the war and was shaken by Thomson's death. Harris joined the army in 1916 and served until early 1918, doing little painting during that period. In the spring, he and his friend Dr. James MacCallum went to the Algoma region of northern Ontario. He returned there seven times during the following six years and was instrumental in encouraging other members of the Group to work in this area. Important though these trips evidently were to him, he produced relatively few paintings of the wilderness subjects. In the immediate postwar years, Harris went through a serious spiritual questioning and artistic re-evaluation. Turning away from landscape, he painted a number of portraits, and although his experience in this genre was limited, a painting such as *Mrs. Oscar Taylor* of 1920 (National Gallery) shows him as an artist in consummate command of his craft.

*A. Y. Jackson, *A Painter's Country* (Toronto: Clarke, Irwin, 1958), p.139.
**Roald Nasgaard, *The Mystic North: Symbolist Landscape Painting in Northern Europe and North America 1890–1940* (Toronto: University of Toronto Press, 1984), pp.169 ff.

Lawren S. Harris
Snow II (1915),
oil on canvas, 120.3 × 127.3 cm.
Purchase, 1916.
Accession No. 1193.

Lawren S. Harris
Shacks (1919),
oil on canvas, 107.9 × 128.0 cm.
Purchase, 1920.
Accession No. 1693.

Lawren S. Harris
North Shore, Lake Superior (1926),
oil on canvas, 102.2 × 128.3 cm.
Purchase, 1930.
Accession No. 3708.

The more radical aspect of Harris's art in these years is evident in his street scenes. *Shacks* of 1919 is one of the most striking of these paintings. Such urban subjects had long interested him, but rather than the moody atmosphere or decorative charm of some of the earlier works, he approaches the subject here with an aggressive palette and an emphatic formalism. He was criticized at the time for choosing working-class areas as his subject. Some modern critics have denied any aspect of social comment in the paintings he made of slum housing in Halifax in 1921, but the character of the paintings stands against this. Moreover, they were made at a time when Harris was giving serious question to the purpose of his work—a self-search that would lead to a striking change in direction.

In 1921, Harris and Jackson went to the north shore of Lake Superior. The harsh beauty of the landscape had a profound effect on Harris and caused a radical change in his painting. He returned to the north shore in each of the next three years, and in 1924 he made his first trip to the Rockies, painting *Maligne Lake, Jasper Park* (National Gallery). In contrast to the richness and surface density of the work of his colleagues, Harris began to make pictures of formal simplicity and restricted colour, reducing the landscape to the interplay of a few boldly described shapes.

Harris's commitment had long been to give expression to his need for spiritual development. This found specific direction when he joined the Theosophical Society around 1918. The theosophic movement had been founded by Madame Blavatsky in 1875 as a search for universal enlightenment, uniting eastern and western spiritual thought. It had a profound effect on many artists and writers in the late nineteenth and early twentieth centuries. Most significant for the visual arts was the relationship of the work of Piet Mondrian and Wassily Kandinsky to the movement's principles. Harris, like so many others, was deeply affected by Kandinsky's essay of 1912, *Concerning the Spiritual in Art*. He began to see the painting of the landscape not as the representation of a particular time and place but as an example of nature as a manifestation of spirit,

where the purpose of art became the vehicle by which to give physical expression to the universal order. His *North Shore, Lake Superior* of 1926 exemplifies this desire, transforming natural events into symbols of mystic truth. The split tree stump may be understood in human terms, a figure of corruption and loss, divided between darkness and light. It stands out against the sky, which itself is divided. To the right is the mass of dark clouds, but to the left the clouds are dissolved by a source of pure, strong light, and the tree stump seems to twist in its roots to reach towards that light.

In the early 1930s, Harris was deeply involved in theosophic studies, frequently lecturing on the subject. He was also in the midst of an emotional crisis, and for a time he stopped painting. In 1934 he divorced his wife and married Bess Housser, recently divorced from Fred Housser, who was the first historian of the Group of Seven. These events caused a social scandal in Toronto, and the Harrises moved to the United States, first to New Hampshire and then, in 1938, to Santa Fe, New Mexico, where Harris became a member of the Transcendental Painting Movement. He moved back to Canada in 1940, settling in Vancouver. He had begun to paint abstracts in 1936, and over the next thirty years he produced some of the most striking and difficult paintings made in Canada. In Vancouver he soon became the centre of a circle of artists and intellectuals, and subsequently took on many responsibilities in relation to cultural policy in Canada, including serving on the Board of Trustees of the National Gallery from 1950 to 1961.

A. Y. Jackson

1882–1974

If Lawren Harris represents the intellect of the Group of Seven, A. Y. Jackson represents its heart. Although the spirit of the Group lay in the painters' immersion in the landscape and in travelling widely across the country, none maintained Jackson's lifelong itinerant habits. And while the professional interests of the others took new directions or moved into other areas, Jackson's commitment to the original purpose of the Group remained essentially unchanged throughout his long career. From the early 1920s, he advocated expanding membership of the Group, and he was a central force in the formation of the Canadian Group of Painters in 1933. He remained an influential figure throughout his life, in his later years becoming both a symbol of the conservatism against which new art in Toronto had to struggle and, to a wider public, the measure of what art in Canada meant.

Jackson's early years were tough. Starting work at the age of twelve, he earned his living in commercial art while taking classes from Edmond Dyonnet and William Brymner in the evenings. He made a brief visit to Europe in 1905. Two years later, spurred by the example of Maurice Cullen and James Wilson Morrice, Jackson went to France to study and work. He was there from 1907 to 1909, with a stint at the Académie Julian, and again from 1911 to early 1913. Back in Montreal, his situation looked bleak until the spring of 1913, when Lawren Harris offered to buy his 1910 painting, *The Edge of the Maple Wood*. Although this is a Canadian scene,

the light and colour of the picture owed much to Jackson's knowledge of Impressionism. J. E. H. MacDonald, however, praised its "native flavour" and Harris said it introduced the "freshest, brightest, most vital Canadian note" in the 1911 Ontario Society of Artists exhibition. Finding in Jackson a kindred spirit, the Toronto painters urged him to join them, which he did in the fall of 1913. His most important painting from the end of that year, its progress carefully watched by Tom Thomson, was *Terre Sauvage*.

This was the first major picture by any member of the Group that related the experience of the wilderness landscape to a sense of style which could stand as an expression of the Canadian experience. Ironically, just a few years earlier, Jackson had considered the Ontario northland an unlikely subject. He wrote in 1910, "It's great country to have a holiday in . . . but it's nothing but little islands covered with scrub and pine trees, and not quite paintable. . . . Sketching simply won't go."*

*Dennis Reid, *The Group of Seven* (Ottawa: National Gallery, 1970), p.34.

A. Y. Jackson
The Edge of the Maple Wood (1910),
oil on canvas, 54.6 × 65.4 cm.
Purchase, 1937.
Accession No. 4298.

A. Y. Jackson
Terre Sauvage (1913),
oil on canvas, 128.8 × 154.4 cm.
Exchange, 1936.
Accession No. 4351.

A. Y. Jackson
Algoma, November (*c*.1935),
oil on canvas, 81.3 × 102.1 cm.
Gift of H. S. Southam, Ottawa, 1945.
Accession No. 4611.

Terre Sauvage was in every sense a pioneering painting—raw in handling and contrived in organization as the artist sought monumentality in structure to match the grandeur of the subject. Yet it was a tough, bold picture, hacking out an image of the northland that sought to transcend individual expression for a larger statement. Jackson had been impressed by the accounts that MacDonald and Harris had given of the Scandinavian exhibition they saw in Buffalo in January 1913, and his painting responds to the particular synthesis of naturalism and decoration that characterized much northern European painting of the turn of the century.

Jackson divided the painting into three regions—rocks, trees, sky—expressing through each a different rhythm of nature's time scale and the passage of the seasons. The unchanging rocks underlie the trees; the evergreens are described by firm, dark outlines, in contrast to the brilliant flashes of the deciduous trees' fall colours. And above them the clouds are filled with a warm light, contrasting with the dark sky that presages the storms of winter. MacDonald gave the picture an even broader context, calling it Mount Ararat because "it looks like the first land that appeared after the Flood subsided."

Terre Sauvage represented an extreme position in Jackson's work. Subsequently, he integrated his more immediate experiences to an underlying sense of the landscape's rhythms. He travelled with Harris on a number of occasions to Algoma, the north shore of Superior, the Rockies, and the Arctic. While Harris was inspired by the monumentality of these places, Jackson seemed less comfortable painting such surroundings; and his best work through the 1920s and 1930s, whether in Algonquin, Algoma, Quebec, or the West, is that which retains a sense of intimacy, even in panoramic views. This is the character of *Algoma, November* (*c*.1935), in which the long, slow curves of the shore and hills are echoed in the cloud layers, while the placid surface of the water, described in short, broken strokes, is played against the light radiating from behind the cloud bank.

Frederick Varley

1881–1969

At a retrospective exhibition of the Group of Seven covering the years from 1919 to 1933, Varley remarked that only he and Harris had moved forward in their art and that he had strong reservations about the direction of Harris's new work. Varley had been an integral part of the Group's emergence, and in 1920, with *Stormy Weather, Georgian Bay*, he painted the most dramatic and, arguably, the most powerful picture to come out of the Group's commitment to the subject of the northern landscape. Yet Varley did not share the belief in a national school of painting founded on the image of a wilderness landscape. His perspective of painting was broader, reaching into the tradition of European painting, and as committed to the human figure as to the landscape.

Varley was a painter's painter—an artist who, far better than most, not only appreciated the potential contained in the material of paint but knew how to exploit its full range. He would make it react to the dynamics of one subject but express the sensitivity of another; there was none of the reticence or politeness that marked the work of some of his contemporaries. Perhaps because of this, full recognition of his achievements came more slowly than to other members of the Group. He once defined the artist as "an outsider, beyond the materialism of his age, one who sees differently—a bloody fool, he cannot be changed. He serves as a foil to others' sanity." It is a definition that goes well with Arthur Lismer's description of him, saying how his red hair "burned like a smouldering torch on top of a head that seemed to have been hacked out with a blunt hatchet."* He suffered for much of his life from extreme financial problems and saw so many projects, bravely entered, founder. His methods of teaching met opposition from colleagues, and he scandalized many by his unconventional lifestyle.

*J. Russell Harper, *Painting in Canada: A History*, 2nd ed. (Toronto: University of Toronto Press, 1977), p.268.

Varley came to Canada in 1912, encouraged by Lismer, after studying in Sheffield and Antwerp, and working as a commercial artist. In Toronto he worked briefly for Grip Ltd. and then for Rous and Mann. He was drawn immediately into a group of young artists, becoming friends with Thomson and meeting MacDonald and Harris at the Arts and Letters Club. His first experience of the northland came in the fall of 1914 when he camped at Canoe Lake in Algonquin Park with Thomson, Lismer, and Jackson. He told their friend Dr. MacCallum, "The country is a revelation to me, and completely bowled me over at first."

The true character of Varley's work emerged after a brief but intense period as an artist for the Canadian War Records Office, when he produced some of the strongest paintings made under that program. He was demobilized in 1920, and a commission for a large-scale mural for the War Records was cancelled for lack of funds; he considered leaving Canada but was persuaded to stay on, with the prospect of receiving some portrait commissions.

In the summer of 1920, he and Lismer went to stay at Dr. MacCallum's cottage on Georgian Bay. During that stay, they made the sketches for what would become, for both of them, their best-known landscape paintings—Lismer's *September Gale, Georgian Bay* and Varley's *Stormy Weather, Georgian Bay*. It has long been suggested that the two men made their sketches for these paintings on the same day, working almost side by side. Yet the results are strikingly different. Lismer's painting, with more than a passing reference to Thomson's *The West Wind*, takes a viewpoint close to the water's edge and shows all the features of the scene— foliage, rocks, waves, clouds—linked into a pattern of curving, stylized forms. In viewpoint and temper,

F. H. Varley
Stormy Weather, Georgian Bay (*c*.1920),
oil on canvas, 132.6 × 162.8 cm.
Purchase, 1921.
Accession No. 1814.

F. H. Varley
Vera (1931),
oil on canvas, 61.0 × 50.6 cm.
Vincent Massey Bequest, 1968.
Accession No. 15559.

Varley's canvas is very close to his preliminary oil sketch. He has taken a higher vantage point than Lismer, and this spreads the horizon and draws our gaze far into the distance, past the broken, rocky islands which characterize that extraordinary coastline. There is nothing decorative about this painting, and its style brilliantly expresses Varley's experience of the day, with the paint laid thickly and worked boldly to form wind-torn foliage, scudding clouds, and driven water.

From the early 1920s, a substantial portion of Varley's output was in portraits, some freely developed, some made on commission. Varley's approach to portraiture owed much to the penetrating characterizations of Augustus John and the example of Oskar Kokoschka, who showed that the painter's prime task, whether making landscape or a portrait, was in the handling of paint.

In 1926, Varley moved to Vancouver to head the painting and drawing department at the Vancouver School of Decorative and Applied Arts. The following year he came to know Vera Weatherbie, a third-year student then aged eighteen. This was the beginning of a ten-year relationship. She became the model for many of his paintings and drawings, none more striking than *Vera*, of 1931.

In Vancouver, Varley found himself part of a small cultural community in which there was a particular interest in Eastern art and religion. His own interest in Buddhism went back to his student days in Antwerp; since the early 1920s, following the colour system developed by Albert Munsell, Varley had developed his own sense of spiritual values to colours. Thus, he equated blue-green with the highest state of spirituality; emerald green with purity; cobalt blue with majesty and mystery; red with earthly and base qualities.

Vera, with its dominant greens modified by blues, reds, and ochres, is a portrait of the person he called "the greatest single influence in my life." The aggressive naturalism of so many of his other paintings, including some of his portraits, is replaced here by a complex formal relationship of curves and shapes: the collar of Vera's blouse is correlated with her hair, the hollow of her neck with her lips; the sweeping lines of her eyebrows and her nose are echoed, inverted, in the sweep of her hair across her forehead. Varley's interpretation really forms a double portrait, divided between left and right. The right side comprises closed forms: the short, high curve of her shoulder, her hair held close to her head, her eye rounded and clear but softened in expression. The left side, by contrast, is open and strongly lit; here her hair sweeps outward, her lips are long and sharply edged, and her eye, formed with narrowing upward curves, glistens darkly beneath a semi-transparent film. And in her face the colour moves from warm ochres on the right to more complex mixtures tending towards green on the left.

The strength of Varley's relationship with Vera was countered by the disintegration of his marriage of twenty years. The pleasure of his teaching at the Vancouver School came to a bitter end in 1933, when severe budget cuts forced him and his colleague Jock Macdonald to resign. Optimistically, they formed the British Columbia College of Arts, but they were able to keep it going only two years. In 1936, Varley left British Columbia on his own for eastern Canada, beginning a period that was to lead him to years of isolation and near destitution. He was at length rescued in the later 1940s by the support of friends and by the broadening recognition among a growing public of the lifelong strength of his art.

Arthur Lismer

1885–1969

Arthur Lismer has few rivals in the development of art education in Canada. Through fifty years of teaching in Halifax, Toronto, and Montreal, he touched the lives and careers of thousands of people. Above all, he is remembered for his work with the many children who attended his classes at the Art Gallery of Toronto and the Montreal Museum of Fine Arts, and at the children's art centres he established. His initiatives, encouraging freedom of expression and contact with original works of art, spurred other educators to develop comparable programs. Warm, outgoing, and witty, Lismer was also much in demand as a lecturer. He became a familiar figure to audiences across the country, speaking on the aims of the Group of Seven in developing a thorough-going Canadian art.

Lismer, like Varley, was born and brought up in Sheffield, England. He attended evening classes at the city's School of Art while apprenticing as a photo-engraver. He followed Fred Varley to the Académie Royale des Beaux-Arts in Antwerp and then returned to Sheffield until he was persuaded by a friend to come to Canada. He arrived early in 1911, and within a month was working at Grip Ltd. alongside J. E. H. MacDonald, Tom Thomson, and Frank Carmichael. He was drawn into the group of like-minded young painters that began to form around MacDonald and Lawren Harris, and from 1913 he was travelling to Georgian Bay and Algonquin Park on sketching trips. Lismer found it a slow and difficult process to break free from his own background in the European landscape painting traditions and respond to the rich, wild character of the northern landscape. His early paintings—such as the two National Gallery pictures, *Georgian Bay*, 1913, and *The Guide's Home, Algonquin*, 1914—are fine adaptations of Impressionism but do not encompass the essence of the places in which he found himself.

Arthur Lismer
The Guide's Home, Algonquin (1914),
oil on canvas, 102.6 × 114.4 cm.
Purchase, 1915.
Accession No. 1155.

Arthur Lismer
September Gale, Georgian Bay (1921),
oil on canvas, 122.4 × 163.0 cm.
Purchase, 1926.
Accession No. 3360.

Lismer was in his mid-thirties when he made the breakthrough that was to set the direction for his mature work. The epitome of this turning point is *September Gale, Georgian Bay* of 1921. In the late summer of 1920, when he and Varley were sketching in Georgian Bay, they made the oil studies that would lead to Lismer's *September Gale, Georgian Bay* and Varley's *Stormy Weather, Georgian Bay*. Both paintings, with a lone tree set on a rocky shore struck by wind-blown water, recall Tom Thomson's *The West Wind*. Varley's painting has often been taken to typify the Group of Seven's approach to the northland, yet in many respects it is Lismer's painting which more directly represents the aims of the Group.

In an article Lismer wrote in 1947, he said that Thomson never sought to tame the wilderness "but only to draw from it its magic of tangle and season, its changing skyline and its quiet or vigorous moods. He gave it a sense of order, revealing the golden thread of aesthetic symbolism—like music, symphonic."* These are telling words, not only for Lismer's perception of Thomson, but also as a reflection on his own work.

*Peter Mellen, *The Group of Seven* (Toronto: McClelland and Stewart, 1970), p.57.

They gain a certain poignancy because, when Thomson was struggling to create finished compositions from his sketches, it was Lismer who advised him to use his skill as a designer as the means of achieving unity. In turn, Lismer responded to Thomson's work, especially to his sense of decorative structure.

It is this that so sharply distinguishes Lismer's painting from Varley's vigorous response to the rawness of nature. In Varley's picture, the tree clings to the land, resisting the wind that is tearing at it. But in Lismer's painting it is the tree, though bowed by the wind, that is the element of stability in the picture, joining earth to sky. It is a painting of order, underpinned by repeated linear forms and complementary shapes: the way the stylized clumps of foliage on the tree are related to the clouds, and how the wind-formed waves meet the curving resistance of the rocks. Through the bold, inter-related, rounded shapes that describe the variety of nature's forms, Lismer seeks the unity to express the "aesthetic symbolism" of his picture.

Emily Carr

1871–1945

Forty-five years after her death, Emily Carr's paintings remain the image of the West Coast. They retain an immediacy of address and have not settled into an historical context, as so much of the Group of Seven work has. This is partly because of her extraordinarily expressive range—one that bridges the directness of, say, Tom Thomson's motifs and the sophisticated pictorial transcendence in Lawren Harris—and it is partly because her pictorial vocabulary, which embraced Fauvism and Cubism, remained closer to current styles than that of the Group of Seven.

Carr was difficult, eccentric, and passionate. She once berated Eric Brown, director of the National Gallery, for the gallery's failure to buy any of her oil paintings: "If the work of an isolated little old woman on the edge of nowhere is too *modern* for the Canadian National Gallery it seems to me it cannot be a very progressive institution."* A few years earlier, when Brown met her to discuss including her work in a National Gallery exhibition, she had to admit that she did not know Canada had a National Gallery and that she had never heard of the Group of Seven. Travelling east for the opening of this exhibition in 1927, she met members of the Group in Toronto. It was from seeing their work and receiving their encouragement that she was inspired to start painting again (for fifteen years she had done little or no painting).

Carr's artistic development had moved slowly; study in San Francisco and England brought her only limited progress. Her work first gained purpose on a trip to Alaska in 1907. When visiting Indian villages along the Northwest Coast, she determined she would make a comprehensive record of the totem poles. (Her first Indian subjects date from a visit to Ucluelet in 1898. A local chief named her Klee Wyck—the laughing one.)

*Doris Shadbolt, *The Art of Emily Carr* (Vancouver: Douglas & McIntyre, 1978), p.108.

She took four trips along the coast between 1908 and 1912. This pattern was broken in 1910–11, when she went to France specifically to find out about the new art being done there. She returned home firmly versed in Post-Impressionist and Fauve painting.

Her visit in 1912 to the Queen Charlotte Islands and the Skeena River resulted in her strongest body of work so far. The watercolour, *Cumshewa*, was made in the studio from site sketches. This Haida village had been abandoned; among the remains was the large carving of a raven raised on a pole; a second carving had rotted away and only its pole survived. The conventional style of Carr's earlier work gave way in this picture to an image of powerful, simplified drawing, which united clouds, mountains, land, and the raven in a curving, dynamic pattern. In her use of colour, she did not transplant a French style to a West Coast subject. Rather, she used what she had learned in France to express a personal response to the density of the rain-soaked landscape of the Queen Charlottes. "The memory of Cumshewa," she wrote in her first book, *Klee Wyck* (1941), "is of a great lonesomeness smothered in a blur of rain." She returned to this image nearly twenty years later in the oil painting *Big Raven* (Vancouver Art Gallery).

Emily Carr
Cumshewa (*c.* 1912),
watercolour over graphite on illustration board, 52.0 × 75.5 cm.
Purchase, 1953.
Accession No. 6103.

Emily Carr
Sky (*c*.1935),
oil on wove paper, 58.7 × 90.7 cm.
Purchase, 1937.
Accession No. 4286.

In 1913, Carr held a large exhibition in Vancouver of her paintings of Indian subjects. The show received a mixed reception and Carr was deeply discouraged. She went back to Victoria and built a small apartment house on land that had been left to her, intending to live from rents and to continue painting. However, she found herself fully occupied in managing the building and turned to other ways, including making pottery, to support herself through hard times. Although she did paint a little and continued to exhibit, her career was essentially in limbo. All this was changed by the visit to eastern Canada in 1927. There followed fourteen years of prolific, urgent, and powerful painting. Her subject matter shifted several times during this period. Starting with Indian subjects, she moved after 1930 to dark, dense paintings of forest interiors, and then, in the mid-1930s, to open, lighter themes. She returned to Indian subjects in her last years.

Sky, of around 1935, is one of a group of paintings of broad open views, linking shore, sea, and sky in a single swirl of movement. Of all the members of the Group of Seven, Lawren Harris was the one to whom she was closest, and they maintained a substantial correspondence. Encouraged by Harris, she struggled to reconcile herself to theosophy before finally rejecting it.

She wrote, "When I tried to see things theosophically I was looking through glasses of cold, hard, inevitable fate, serene perhaps but cold, unjoyous and unmoving. Seeing things the Christ way, things are dipped in love."[**]

Nevertheless, she was influenced by the moves towards abstraction in Harris's painting and found common ground with him in the drive to express in painting the unity of all things, physical and spiritual. In *Sky*, the horizon and the distant mountains seem to curve upward, countering the curvature of the earth, as if they are centred on the source of light. The clouds, too, ring this central source from which beams of light spread to engage every part of the picture. Although references to the natural world remain, the painting is close to abstraction, not in the sense of moving away from the world but by moving towards an enveloping light-filled centre.

[**]*Ibid.*, p.58

Frank H. Johnston

1888–1949

At the first exhibition of the Group of Seven in May 1920, Frank Johnston hung more work than any of the other artists. It was the only Group of Seven exhibition in which he participated. In 1924, returning to Toronto after three years teaching in Winnipeg, the news was reported of his resignation from the Group. In an interview given at the time, Johnston downplayed the significance of the event: "I was never a member of the school of seven in the sense of taking a formal oath of allegiance to an art brotherhood or of subscribing to rigid doctrines. They were my friends. I shared their enthusiasm for new ideas and new methods."*

Johnston had become friends with future members of the Group during his time working for the commercial art company of Grip Ltd. But in the crucial early years of the Group's formation, from around 1911, Johnston was in the United States studying and working as a commercial artist. He returned to Toronto in 1915, and in the last months of the war he did some work for the Canadian War Records at flying training schools near Toronto. The most striking painting to come from this was the National War Museum's *Beamsville* of 1918–19, showing aircraft from the School of Aerial Gunnery.

Johnston's most important involvement with the work of the Group of Seven came through the three Algoma trips in which he participated between 1918 and 1920. These expeditions had an important impact on the work of Harris and MacDonald, the two members of the Group with whom Johnston was closest, and they were the source of Johnston's best paintings. His most successful major work was *Fire-swept, Algoma* of 1920. In this picture Johnston transcended the immediate view, reaching towards an image that revealed the natural cycle of destruction and regeneration. The raw, burnt hillside is a stark contrast to the distant, richly wooded hills. Yet as we look closely, we see how the dark slashes of the charred trees seem to merge with the foliage of the trees on the far hills. Reciprocating this, the short, vertical strokes that describe the distant trees are repeated in the foreground in the bright strokes of green that indicate the first stages of regrowth after the fire.

This painting stands in strong contrast to one from a very similar viewpoint that A. Y. Jackson made some months earlier, *First Snow, Algoma*. Against Johnston's broad, panoramic sweep, Jackson paints a dramatic clash of forces—the devastation of the landscape perhaps holding memories for him of the shell-blasted landscapes he had painted in wartime France.

*Peter Mellen, *The Group of Seven* (Toronto: McClelland and Stewart, 1970), p.136.

Frank H. Johnston
Fire-swept, Algoma (1920),
oil on canvas, 127.5 × 167.5 cm.
Purchase, 1920.
Accession No. 1694.

Johnston left Toronto in 1921 to become principal of the Winnipeg School of Art, remaining there until 1924. He took up teaching again in 1929 when MacDonald, then principal of the Ontario College of Art, brought him onto the staff. Johnston continued his prolific output of work, enjoying considerable popular and commercial success, though the decorative styles he favoured took

him away from the challenges which marked the developing work of the Group of Seven. He remained a close friend of MacDonald; his differences with his former colleagues centred on Jackson. Jackson's strong commitment to the Group's ideas on how Canadian painting should develop clashed with Johnston's demand for independence. Johnston criticized the Group for making the works it exhibited have a common look. His argument was weakened, however, by the Group's individual strengths from the 1920s on, particularly in Harris, Varley, and Jackson, and by the fact that his independence of attitude was not matched by a creative direction of equivalent conviction.

A. Y. Jackson
First Snow, Algoma (1919–20),
oil on canvas, 106.7 × 127 cm.
The McMichael Conservation Collection of Art, Kleinburg.
Gift of Mr. Percy Hilborn Preston.

David B. Milne

1882–1953

In 1924, the National Gallery purchased six watercolours from David Milne, the first works of the artist to enter the collection. Today, the gallery possesses the largest collection of Milne's work, including substantial donations from the Vincent Massey Bequest and the Estate of Douglas Duncan, as well as the majority of pieces that Milne made for the Canadian War Records in 1918–19. The fullness of the collection belies Milne's long years of struggle when he sought to make a living from his art—an art outside the mainstream, just as he himself remained independent of groups and movements.

Milne's working career was divided almost equally between Canada and the United States. Brought up in rural Ontario, he first took classes by correspondence and then, in 1903, went to New York to study, enrolling at the Art Students League. More important than formal instruction was the friendship with other young artists and the wide range of art that was to be seen in New York's museums and galleries. By the early 1910s, Milne's work was gaining some attention, and he was one of only two Canadians included in the 1913 Armory Show in New York. The mature development of his art began when he left the city to work in relative isolation in the country. From 1916 to 1929, with the exception of his army service and a winter in Ottawa in 1923–24, he lived in the Berkshires and upstate New York. When in 1929 he returned to Canada, he chose small communities north of Toronto: Palgrave, Six Mile Lake near Orillia, Uxbridge, and finally Bancroft.

His independence was marked even before his move to Boston Corners, N.Y., in 1916, frustrating attempts to describe a specific line of influence. Links to the Late Impressionist members of the Ten American Artists and to Maurice Prendergast suggest an area of interest rather than a direction. Fauvism made its impact, in particular the colour of Matisse—who had his first American show at Stieglitz's "291" gallery in 1908—and Raoul Dufy's drawing and balance of colour and open spaces. The overall patterning and colour structure of Bonnard and Vuillard cannot be overlooked, while Milne's early etchings show a debt to the line and atmosphere of Whistler's prints. Yet it was a particular and individual approach that led him to make a watercolour such as his *Stippled Pattern No. 6* of 1914. What is striking here is not so much the closeness of viewpoint that suggests abstraction, but the intensity with which Milne sought the basis for a pictorial construction that was directly related to the marks and strokes he set down. This small picture has both an analysis and a synthesis that are invented and not derived.

David B. Milne
Painting Place No. 3 (1930),
oil on canvas, 51.3 × 66.4 cm.
Vincent Massey Bequest, 1968.
Accession No. 15520.

The working isolation Milne came to desire reflected the powerful self-criticism in his mature art. There is no better example of his pictorial process than in the composition *Painting Place*, of which he made three painted versions and three print versions over a four-year period. He made the first painting very quickly in August 1926, responding to the impression that the view from a promontory overlooking Big Moose Lake, New York, had made on him. "The moving scene within is passable," he wrote to a friend, "but it is the frame that grips your heart. I didnt [*sic*] notice that there was a frame at first, not until I had curled up on a raincoat for an hours [*sic*] nap in the hot sun. The first blink on waking, before I lifted my head, introduced the frame. . . . It is often hard to tell what leads one to see a picture. In this case it was undoubtedly the vigor of the shapes—rather the vigorous markings of them with black.''*

*Rosemarie Tovell, *David Milne: Painting Place. Masterpieces in the National Gallery of Canada, No. 8* (Ottawa: National Gallery, 1976), p.12.

David B. Milne
Stippled Pattern No. 6 (1914),
watercolour over graphite on wove paper, 67.0 × 46.0 cm.
Purchase, 1987.
Accession No. 29700.

The view across the lake is seen through a screen of spruces, with the shattered trunk of a tree close to us marking the left edge. In the foreground lie a painter's box and brushes, a glass jar and other bottles; the view and evidence of the painter's presence are inseparable.

Finishing the first painting, Milne began the second but abandoned it with the far shore uncompleted. The following year he made a small drypoint print of the subject, and then he set the idea aside for two years before coming back to it in a second, larger print. The success of this one led him to rework the unfinished painting and then, in 1930, to paint the third version. Finally, the editor of an American book, *The Colophon*, asked him to make an edition of the large print for inclusion in the book. Over an eight-month period, he pulled more than three thousand impressions for the publication. It appeared in 1931 under the title *Hilltop*.

Painting Place No. 3 is a mature, unified picture, limited to black and white and three colours—green, red, and purple. As is often true of Milne's work, the composition is relatively rigid, here forming a gridlike structure. Within this is an evenly distributed balance of black and white, opened by a sparing use of the three colours to give fullness to the elements. The use of the colours and the range of values in relation to their shape and position within the picture are susceptible to close analysis, but the extraordinary aspect of the painting is how we perceive it as neither rigid nor limited in colour. The freedom of Milne's drawing, giving texture and atmosphere to the contours, combined with the range of tonal values, leaves us with the image of a picture that is full and round in colour.

Bertram Brooker

1888–1955

Bertram Brooker remains a puzzling figure in the story of Canadian art. Energetic and innovative, he cut across the grain. He was successful in the various activities he took up and yet, as an artist, he leaves us with a sense of disappointment, of a promise not wholly realized. Brooker was in his late thirties when he began to paint seriously. He had been living in Toronto for five years, having moved there from Winnipeg to edit the trade journal of the Canadian advertising industry. In 1930, after four years devoted to painting and free-lance writing, he returned to advertising work. Those four years coincided with a brief but exciting period for the small circle of Torontonians who were interested in advanced art.

Brooker was drawn into the artistic and intellectual milieu of the Group of Seven and held his first exhibition at the Arts and Letters Club in 1927. His decision to start painting seems to have been sparked by his friendship with Lawren Harris and Fred Housser, who impressed him with their arguments promoting a type of Canadian painting that was a pursuit of the Canadian spirit and not simply a reflection of scenery. Within the Group of Seven, Harris was taking a progressively radical line, linked to his theosophic convictions. Brooker expressed similar interests. He wrote of seeking in painting "manifestations of a great unified reach of being whose every part depends upon, or gives birth to every other part, in an endless and subtly interrelated 'becoming.'"

Between 1926 and 1930, he sought to realize this in a series of abstract paintings and drawings—the first ever exhibited by a Canadian—the most powerful being *Sounds Assembling* of 1928 (Winnipeg Art Gallery) and *Alleluiah* of 1929.

Personal in their intent, these images drew on a number of sources. Harris probably encouraged Brooker to read Wassily Kandinsky's *Concerning the Spiritual in Art*. Throughout this essay, Kandinsky parallels painting and music, both in general terms and specifically by relating colours to sounds and feelings—references which Brooker found compelling. The formal structure of the paintings is reminiscent of the American futuristic painter, Joseph Stella, and the abstractions of the Italian futurists, Umberto Boccioni, Carlo Carrà, and Luigi Russolo. Brooker's interest in theosophy would probably also have led him to know the descriptions of "thought forms," set out in the writings of Annie Besant and C. W. Leadbeater, in which forms and colours are shown as emanations of spiritual and emotional characteristics.

Alleluiah is a cosmic landscape. Horizontally, it is divided into three planes, which are distinct in colour and shape: green below; then snowy white tinged with blue; and above this, arcs of blue, ranging from the lightest to the darkest hues. Through these levels, forms predominantly in black and white are brought into conflict: white emanating from a starlike burst of intense light; black in a group of bars or columns. The force of light bursts out, breaking and scattering the black bars, symbolizing "Alleluiah!"—the cry of praise, the triumph of the pure spirit over the imprisonment of darkness.

In 1930, quite suddenly, Brooker reversed direction in his work. The reasons remain obscure, but two factors have been suggested.* The stance he took in his work led him to receive considerable criticism, and the broad opposition to abstract art included some people

*Dennis Reid, *Bertram Brooker*, Canadian Artists Series, No.1 (Ottawa: National Gallery, 1979), p.14.

he counted as colleagues. The second factor was his friendship with Lionel LeMoine FitzGerald. He met FitzGerald in 1929 on a trip to Winnipeg (despite the many years Brooker lived in Toronto, he always considered himself a Winnipeger). He was deeply impressed by the man and his work, and a lifelong friendship developed, based on occasional meetings and correspondence. Almost immediately, Brooker's work showed the influence of FitzGerald's cool and precise realism. He told FitzGerald that he might in time return to abstract art, and in the late 1930s he did make some moves in this direction. But he never recaptured the daring or excitement of those first works.

Bertram Brooker
Alleluiah (c.1929),
oil on canvas, 123.0 × 123.3 cm.
Purchase, 1969.
Accession No. 15812.

Edwin Holgate

1892–1977

In a number of respects, Holgate's place within Canadian art history is a curious one. He was closely associated with some of the major movements of the day—he joined the Group of Seven in 1930 and was later a member of the Canadian Group of Painters—yet he was never central to these movements. He was equally comfortable in both the English and the French cultural communities of Montreal without being a demonstrative bridge between them. He was an active member of the Montreal art scene through the 1920s and 1930s as a painter, printmaker, and teacher; he supported John Lyman's efforts to start an art school in 1932, but was conspicuously absent from Lyman's Contemporary Arts Society formed in 1939. When he returned to Montreal in 1944 from service abroad with the Canadian War Art Program, he felt out of place in regard to the directions that serious art in the city was taking. In 1946 he moved out to Morin Heights in the Laurentians, glad of the freedom to paint, and he gradually withdrew from regular exhibiting.

Holgate studied briefly with Maurice Cullen and then at the Art Association of Montreal with William Brymner. Given this background, Paris was inevitably the next move, and he made his first trip there in 1912, arriving back in Montreal in 1915. He spent three years in France with the army during the First World War and was back in Paris again in 1920, studying with a Russian painter, Adolf Milman. Holgate met and became friends with James Wilson Morrice, and his work soon showed Morrice's influence.

After Holgate's return to Montreal in 1922, his paintings evinced the boldness of form, simplicity of detail, and forceful colour that characterized his mature style. His serious application to landscape painting began in 1924 when he went sketching along the north shore of the St. Lawrence with A. Y. Jackson, Clarence Gagnon, and Albert Robinson. He, Jackson, and Robinson went again to the north shore in 1926, and later that year he went with Jackson and the anthropologist Marius Barbeau to the Skeena River district in northern British Columbia. Out of this trip came the strong *Totem Poles, Gitsegiuklas* of 1927 (National Gallery). Although Holgate's early landscapes showed the influence of

Jackson, his viewpoint was invariably tighter and closer, his light direct and lacking in atmosphere, and his colour high-keyed. His approach to figure paintings was similar, and he linked the two genres in a number of paintings of female nudes in landscape settings, such as the National Gallery's *Nude in a Landscape* of 1930.

Holgate was second only to Varley as a portrait painter, and his *Ludivine*, painted around 1930, stands as the finest painting he ever made. In 1929 he went along the north shore to Labrador, and in the Quebec village of Natashquan he made studies of Ludivine. The girl's mother had recently died—Ludivine is shown still in mourning—and as the eldest child, the responsibility of caring for the family had fallen to her. Holgate paints with a direct, searching light, bringing the features of the girl's face, neck, and hands into a sculpted relief that casts a heavy shadow behind her. Holgate once said that his long admiration of Paul Cézanne's work arose from the artist's sense of structure, yet much of the brilliance in *Ludivine* is compositional. The girl is placed just off-centre—the centre line of the picture passes through her left eye—and the dark shadow behind her seems to draw her farther to the left. This tension, emphasized by the slight turn of her shoulders, tempers her appearance of strength and composure; for what we see in her is both the girl and the woman, her childhood not yet lost behind the adulthood that circumstance has cast on her. Holgate underlines this ambiguity by posing her so that the curved back of the settee on one side contrasts with the sharp, scalloped decoration on the other. The force of the picture is made all the more striking by Holgate's bold use of colour. The green and turquoise, because of their contrast with the flesh tones, add strength to them, projecting the figure into the space of our attention.

Edwin Holgate
Ludivine (*c*.1930),
oil on canvas, 76.3 × 63.9 cm.
Vincent Massey Bequest, 1968.
Accession No. 15478.

Lionel LeMoine FitzGerald

1890–1956

Writing about the late work of Cézanne, the critic Lawrence Gowing said, "We do not have the critical equipment to evaluate the existential tenor of a formal style." It is a perception, finely observed, that comes to mind when looking at the drawings and paintings of Lionel LeMoine FitzGerald, for there is the fear that any analysis of FitzGerald's work—whether concentrating on formal structure or the representational aspects— will only serve to pull apart the tissue of the image.

In July 1932, FitzGerald was invited to join the Group of Seven. It was no doubt a sincere gesture, but it was a curious one nevertheless. It had no effective meaning, for the Group had held its last exhibition the year before. Furthermore, FitzGerald's work was very different in both character and spirit from the dense, richly painted surfaces that were typical of the Group. The Group of Seven painters were, of course, looking to break out from the criticism that no matter how national their aspirations were, they were viewed as a Toronto enterprise. In approaching FitzGerald, however, they were drawing on someone who made no conces- sion to the fact that everything he did was in response to his immediate surroundings.

FitzGerald was born in Winnipeg, and he spent all his life there except for the year 1921–22 when, at the age of thirty-one, he went to study at the Art Students League in New York. He was impressed by Frank John- ston, who was in Winnipeg heading the School of Art from 1921 to 1924. FitzGerald joined the faculty of the school in 1924 and became its principal five years later. His closest artistic colleagues, however, were Fritz Brandtner (who lived in Winnipeg for a few years before moving to Montreal in 1934) and Toronto-based Bertram Brooker, whom FitzGerald first met in 1929.

FitzGerald's work, with its emphasis on simplified, formal construction, appears related to the paintings that Lawren Harris made in the 1920s after his first trips to Lake Superior. Yet the thinking and artistic purpose of the two men differed widely. Harris sought the vastness and grandeur of Lake Superior and the Rockies because they inspired him as being openings onto the infinite. FitzGerald was always concerned with the intimate scale of familiar places, with the inexhaustible range of subjects that surrounded him. The character of his interests and his quiet pursuit of them was well summed up when he said, "It is evident that no one object can be segregated in space without the feeling of something around it, and usually it is associated with other objects. The appreciation of the relation of one object to another and their effect on one another will help to suggest the solidity of each."* It is a disarmingly simple statement, yet one that clearly describes his approach, an approach arising not from a grand, sweeping vision but from the gradual linking of one small area to another.

Drawing was FitzGerald's main technique; finely worked, subtle, undemonstrative. Of his relatively few paintings, *Doc Snyder's House* of 1931 is rare both in scale and complexity. The simplification of the forms is accompanied by a consciously limited range of colour in order to create those few contrasts that will express the absolute clarity of prairie winter light. The structure of the painting is firm but understated; we are hardly aware of how our attention is drawn to the centre of the picture, and that the area around the bird-feeder, the window, and the top of the fence is the measure by which we move out and around, and to which we return. From this core of order—and held to the surface by the brilliance of the light—our eye is taken by the rhythm of the picture, which is played out in the contrasts between the rigid geometry of the houses and the eccentric curves and angles of the trees.

Towards the end of his life, FitzGerald did make some abstract pictures, but it would be wrong to think of them as the culminating point of an inevitable process. The essence of his work, no matter how "formal" it became, lay in the fullness of perception of that endless potential in the relationship of light and shape which comprises our immediate experience of the world.

L. L. FitzGerald 1890–1956: A Memorial Exhibition (Ottawa: National Gallery, 1958).

L. L. FitzGerald
Doc Snyder's House (1931),
oil on canvas, 74.9 × 85.1 cm.
Gift of P. D. Ross, Ottawa, 1932.
Accession No. 3993.

Carl Schaefer

born 1903

The Group of Seven painters had sought—and, in their own terms, had given expression to—a singularly Canadian vision. Among their successors through the 1930s and 1940s, it was the strong painters who used this as a basis to build from and to react against, while others simply preserved and perpetuated the image. The formation of the Canadian Group of Painters in 1933 partly fulfilled some of the Group of Seven's wishes to see their initiatives gain a broader base. The new group did achieve the sense of a national forum—albeit an incomplete one—at a time when the visual arts were receiving little encouragement or support. But while the Group of Seven members travelled widely, this was not possible for most of their younger contemporaries. This tended to emphasize regional issues, although there was never in Canada a movement comparable to American Regionalism. Nevertheless, some tough painting came out of the harsh years of the Depression, one of the strongest artists being Carl Schaefer, who forged a personal image of landscape painting.

Schaefer grew up on a farm owned by his grandparents near Hanover, Ontario. His boyhood interest in art, developed through book and magazine illustrations, led him to enroll at the Ontario College of Art in 1921. Arthur Lismer and J. E. H. MacDonald were among his teachers, and the example of A. Y. Jackson and Lawren Harris also played an important role in his artistic development. With this background, it is not surprising that Schaefer's early work reflected the influence of the Group of Seven.

Through the 1930s, Schaefer was teaching part-time in Toronto, but during the holidays he and his family moved back to the Hanover farm. The reasons for going back to the country were economic, but Schaefer soon recognized that the vital aspects of his personal style and expression were most fully realized by choosing his subjects from this place to which he had lifelong ties. Schaefer admired the work of Charles Burchfield and found himself sympathetic to the American's often pessimistic views of small-town and rural life. By his work through the 1930s, Schaefer distanced himself from the vision of the land which the Group of Seven had established. Whereas they had raised the northern wilderness to a symbol of national expression, Schaefer emphasized the harshness of rural conditions and the reality for the thousands of farmers who made their living from cultivating the land. His image of the land was best expressed in a number of panoramic paintings of the fields around Hanover, such as his *Storm over the Fields* of 1937 (Art Gallery of Ontario). Rather than

glorifying the wilderness as the Group of Seven had done, Schaefer focused on the work that must precede the reward of the crops and emphasized farming people's dependence on the uncertainties of nature.

The metaphoric character of Schaefer's work is nowhere more evident than in *Ontario Farmhouse* of 1934. The image of the house, isolated against the sky by a low viewpoint, brings to mind the paintings of the American artist, Edward Hopper. But in contrast to Hopper's unsettling sense of abandonment, Schaefer's house is a symbol of security and stability. The rich, fruitful fields press up close to it, and the potential for failure, marked by the barren tree, is relegated to a minor position. Light radiates over the whole scene, and the golds and greens and warm ochres in the fields find their counterpart in the colours of the house. Schaefer said that he was not painting for posterity. Certainly, *Ontario Farmhouse*, linking nostalgia and optimism, stands bravely as a painting of its time.

Carl Schaefer
Storm over the Fields (1937),
oil on canvas, 68.6 × 94.6 cm.
Art Gallery of Ontario, Toronto.
Gift from J. S. McLean Canadian Fund, 1964.

Carl Schaefer
Ontario Farmhouse (1934),
oil on canvas, 106.5 × 124.7 cm.
Gift of Floyd S. Chalmers, Toronto, 1969.
Accession No. 15845.

John Lyman

1886–1967

In 1988 the Estate of Dr. Max Stern presented the National Gallery with John Lyman's *On the Beach (St-Jean-de-Luz)*, made in 1929–30. There is a nice irony in the fact that one of the best paintings Lyman ever made should find a permanent home in the gallery's collections, for in his lifetime Lyman came into bitter conflict with H. O. McCurry, a director of the National Gallery.

Lyman holds a special place in the emergence of modernist art in Canada. Through the 1930s and 1940s, he did more than any other individual—by example, education, and organization—to encourage artists, collectors, and art institutions in Montreal into an awareness of and participation in the broad movement of modernist art. He had spent his early adult life in Paris and in 1909 had studied with Henri Matisse. Although his time in the Matisse atelier was brief, the example of the Fauvist painter made a deep and lasting impression on him. In 1913, Lyman showed some of his Fauvist paintings at the Art Association of Montreal spring exhibition. He was severely shaken by the harshness of the criticism levelled against him; even in old age, he would recall the experience with undimmed anger. He returned to live in Montreal in 1931 and immediately assumed a position of leadership in encouraging other artists to experiment in their work and to act collectively against the resistance to innovation. He gave public voice to his beliefs through critical writing, most importantly through a column he wrote in the *Montrealer* between 1936 and 1940. His major organizational move came with his formation of the Contemporary Arts Society in 1939.

The society was founded to foster discussion and education on art as well as to mount exhibitions. From the start, Lyman was anxious to include both English- and French-speaking artists, and a category of "associate" membership was created to include writers, collectors, and interested members of the public. Lectures were held and exhibitions arranged. Society members boycotted the 1943 and 1944 Art Association of Montreal spring exhibitions, successfully forcing changes in the jury system.

In 1942, Lyman was closely involved with an exhibition, "Aspects of Contemporary Painting in Canada," in which Contemporary Arts Society members were well represented, while prominent artists from the Canadian Group of Painters were excluded. The exhibition was shown at the Addison Gallery of American Art in Andover, Massachusetts. It was also booked into the Metropolitan Museum in New York, but the booking was cancelled after pressure from "official channels in Ottawa." It seems that H. O. McCurry and A. Y. Jackson were responsible for bringing this pressure to bear. (Lyman had never concealed his opinion that the support the Group of Seven received and the power the Canadian Group of Painters enjoyed had an inhibiting effect on the development of Canadian art.)

A curious outcome of Lyman's vigorous advocacy of modernist art in Quebec was that the nurturing of greater openness helped to foster divisions within advanced artistic circles as his approach was overtaken by ideas more radical than his own. Lyman was a formalist, a purist in the *art pour l'art* sense. This was a direction of modernism that came under attack from Paul-Émile Borduas and the younger Automatistes. In addition, the Contemporary Arts Society itself became a forum for political and ideological differences. At its dissolution in 1948, it was divided into three principal groups: Lyman and the older, predominantly English-speaking artists; Borduas and the Automatistes; Alfred Pellan and the *Prisme d'yeux*.

While Lyman was the dominant personality during these crucial years, he did not give a commanding example in his own work. He was an uneven artist whose paintings too often seemed to be an echo of those he admired, rather than a voice that was uniquely his own. This is not to accuse him of reticence; his 1936 painting, *Lady with a White Collar* (National Gallery), is aggressive in drawing and colour. But occasionally, as with *On the Beach (St-Jean-de-Luz)*, he made a picture about which we want to say that here, both in style and subject, is the essential Lyman. This painting has a rare sparkle; and the interlocking of coloured shapes, boldly formed, exemplifies that purist approach which Lyman so fervently advocated.

John Lyman
On the Beach (St-Jean-de-Luz) (1929–30),
oil on paper, mounted on canvas, 45.6 × 55.5 cm.
Presented by the executors of Dr. Max Stern, 1988, in
accordance with his wishes.
Accession No. 30182.

Prudence Heward

1896–1947

Through the 1920s and 1930s there were various groups of artists within the English-speaking community in Montreal. In general, their work is not widely known. This is partly because of the attention given to the Group of Seven during these years and partly because these artists came to represent a reaction to the developments among young French-speaking artists. Until John Lyman returned to Canada and moved towards forming the Contemporary Arts Society, the most important activity centred on the Beaver Hall Hill Group. The idea of the group appears to have originated with Randolph Hewton, a friend of A. Y. Jackson, and it took its lead from the Group of Seven while tracing its origins to the fact that its members had all been students of William Brymner. The group lasted as such for only two years (1920–22), but the friendships among the members continued, and other artists were gradually drawn into the circle. The most notable and significant aspect of the group was that many of the members were women, comprising, even if informally, the most substantial grouping of women professional artists in Canada to that time.

Prudence Heward became associated with the group in the later 1920s. She had studied with Brymner and also with Maurice Cullen. Her work was interrupted by service with the Red Cross in London during the First World War. After the war, she continued her studies with Hewton and then with the Fauvist painter, Charles Guérin, at the Académie Colarossi in Paris. Her work developed slowly and quietly through the 1920s, and she first received serious notice when she won the Willingdon Arts Competition in 1929 with her *Girl on a Hill*, 1928, which is now in the National Gallery collection. From that point on, her work gained increasing recognition—if not in a public sense, then at least from her peers. She joined the Canadian Group of Painters in 1933 and served for a time as vice-president. In 1939 she was one of the few Beaver Hall Hill artists to become a member of Lyman's Contemporary Arts Society.

Heward painted both landscape and figure subjects, often combining the two genres, her greatest strength being her paintings of women. Her nude in a landscape—*Girl under a Tree* of 1931 (National Gallery)—elicited from John Lyman the comment that it was "Bouguereau nude against Cézanne background."* Yet the painting had daring and force, in contrast to similar subjects being painted by Edwin Holgate. Many of her paintings were titled in a general sense: *Dark Girl, Italian Woman, Girl in a Window, The Farmer's Daughter*. Others identified their models simply by the first name, such as *Rollande*.

Made in 1929, when Heward was beginning to attract attention, *Rollande* is a strong, mature picture. It is a large painting—the figure is full-size—and is powerful and direct. That directness comes in the reduction of the elements to their essential shapes and in the balance between the woman and the context of her life. Her pose is set in rhythm with the diagonals of the fence against which she stands, a relationship that implies both activity and firmness. Her head and shoulders are held strong and square; and Heward has modelled the head with a minimum of detail, contrasting the vital colouring of the woman's face with the sharp greens behind her and the lilac of her smock.

*Charles C. Hill, *Canadian Painting in the Thirties* (Ottawa: National Gallery of Canada, 1975), p.42.

Prudence Heward
Rollande (1929),
oil on canvas, 139.9 × 101.7 cm.
Purchase, 1930.
Accession No. 3700.

Paraskeva Clark

1898–1986

'They didn't even paint still life . . . nothing but landscape, landscape, landscape.'* Paraskeva Clark, looking back over almost fifty years of life in Canada, recalled her disbelief in finding that in the early 1930s the leadership of Canadian art was held by artists dedicated to painting the wilderness landscape. Clark herself later came to paint landscape frequently, but her *cri de coeur* was really directed elsewhere: first, at the way so much in contemporary Canadian art simply ignored what had been happening in European art for more than thirty years; second, that the preoccupation with landscape marked a lack of commitment to the larger human issues that were so evident at the time, with economic disaster at home and political upheaval abroad. It was a mature sense of commitment and a position from which she was able to understand the meaning of the tumultuous events that had reformed the world in which she had grown up.

Born in 1898 in St. Petersburg (which was renamed Petrograd in 1914 and Leningrad in 1924), Clark turned to art after her attempts to work in theatre were thwarted. She studied part-time at the Petrograd Academy of Arts from 1916, becoming a full-time student after the Russian Revolution, when the academy was reopened as the Free Art Studios. She studied with Kuzma Petrov-Vodkin, and his teaching, particularly with regard to the development of pictorial space, remained a decisive influence on her work. In later life, she would say little about the harsh years of the war and the immediate post-revolution period. She gained freedom from that in 1923, but only under tragic circumstances. In 1922 she married Oreste Allegri, whose family was in the theatre-design business, both in Petrograd and Paris. The following year Allegri was accidentally killed, and Paraskeva and her infant son went to Paris to live with Allegri's parents. In 1929 she met Philip Clark, an accountant from Toronto. Two years later she married him and moved to Canada. Philip Clark was a member of the Arts and Letters Club, and he introduced his wife to the circle of artists he knew. She was encouraged to start painting again, for she had done little work since leaving Petrograd.

*Mary E. MacLachlan, *Paraskeva Clark: Paintings and Drawings* (Halifax: Dalhousie Art Gallery, 1982), p.21.

Among her most striking paintings are a number of self-portraits made between 1925 and 1942. The most powerful is the *Self-Portrait* of 1933, also known as *Myself* and *Woman in Black*. The elegance of the picture, apparently so easily accomplished, arises from the fine balance between the pose of the figure and the upright architectural elements which fan away from the vertical from right to left. Within these contrasting movements and the rich black tones, our attention is focused on Clark's face, with its direct and forthright gaze and strongly sculpted features. The painting is one of the most powerful figure paintings in Canadian art.

In the course of the later 1930s, Clark became increasingly politically active. In this she was inspired by Norman Bethune, whom she first met in 1936 when he was working in support of the Republicans in the Spanish Civil War. She began to make work that expressed her left-wing thinking, and she found new ways to relate to memories of her Russian past, notably in the 1937 painting, *Petroushka*. After the Nazi invasion of Russia in 1941, she worked energetically—in her painting and also by writing, lecturing, and organizing— to foster support in Canada for the Russian war effort. After the war, she supported the progressive movement in Toronto that was initiated by the Painters Eleven. In her own work, however, she concentrated for the most part on landscape and still life, saying in 1960 that she was "too old now to start following the young."

Paraskeva Clark
Myself (1933),
oil on canvas, 101.6 × 76.7 cm.
Purchase, 1974.
Accession No. 18311.

Miller Brittain

1912–1968

The Regionalist movement in the United States between the two world wars had no equivalent in Canada. American Regionalism was a manifestation of national identity, reflecting the politics of isolationism and the desire for cultural decentralization. In Canada, the situation was one of isolation rather than isolationism, and the emphasis on national identity meant the centralized version of the Group of Seven. It is interesting that many artists who did not see matters in the Group of Seven's terms in fact turned to the United States for their point of reference. The work and career of Miller Brittain is an example of this.

Brittain was born in Saint John, New Brunswick. His life and work were centred on that city, yet his training and his essential artistic contacts were in the United States. He studied at the Art Students League in New York from 1930 to 1932, a time that coincided with a growing emphasis on American subjects as the effects of the Great Depression took hold. Brittain was drawn to the subjects of urban working life found in the paintings of Reginald Marsh, Raphael Soyer, Edward Laning, and Isabel Bishop—all of whom had studied at the Art Students League and would return to teach there.

Through the later 1930s and early 1940s, Brittain produced a series of powerfully expressive paintings and drawings of working-class life in Saint John, with occasional forays into social satire. His compositions are often awkward, crammed with clumsy heavy-featured people, their dark confusion sometimes surprisingly lit by flashes of bright colour. The best of them, such as *The Rummage Sale* of 1940, are strikingly honest in characterization, and they hold a fine balance between the turmoil of a crowd and the individuals who comprise it. Here, the overall impression is of an ungainly scramble: the women push and shove in their grab for bargains; we catch the eye of a woman slyly delighted at the shapeless garment she has managed to grasp; and on the right, two children glance at us with expressions of blank distress at the behaviour of their elders.

Miller Brittain
The Rummage Sale (1940),
oil on masonite, 63.4 × 50.8 cm.
Purchase, 1976.
Accession No. 18557.

Brittain showed *The Rummage Sale* at the Contemporary Arts Society's 1940 exhibition, "Art of Our Day in Canada," and he exhibited twice more with the society. In 1941 he received a major mural commission for the Saint John Tuberculosis Hospital and made eleven powerfully drawn large-scale cartoons for it before the project was cancelled. In 1942 he joined the Royal Canadian Air Force, and he flew operationally as a bomb aimer in 1944–45, gaining a commission and being awarded the Distinguished Flying Cross. He joined the Canadian War Art Program shortly before the end of the war and worked for it until his discharge in 1946.

At first, after the war, Brittain seemed to pick up his painting where he had left off, but the character and style of his work soon changed. He began to make pictures with religious themes and developed a quasi-Surrealist manner of painting in bright, often strident colouring. It is intensely personal difficult work that has not found an audience. These inward-looking paintings affirm the sense of isolation that Brittain had long experienced—an isolation born from his bitter feelings of being disregarded by the "art establishment." And, indeed, the powerful reflections Brittain made of life in Saint John have still not been given the broad appreciation they deserve.

J. W. G. (Jock) Macdonald

1897–1960

Jock Macdonald's career in many respects is the epitome of the early development of modernist art in Canada. Superficially, this seems a paradox, since Macdonald formed a bridge between the Group of Seven and Painters Eleven, even though it was partly the inhibiting influence of the Group of Seven that encouraged Painters Eleven to come into being. The significant issue, however, is that when Macdonald began painting, the leading mode of painting in Canada was already thirty years behind European art; when he died in 1960, his recent work was responsive to some of the most advanced painting of the day, which was then coming from New York.

Born in Scotland, Macdonald arrived in Canada in 1926 to become head of design at the Vancouver School of Decorative and Applied Arts. The same year, Fred Varley arrived at the school as head of the painting and drawing department. Varley was the first of a series of people who were to have a major impact on Macdonald. He tutored Macdonald in oil painting and encouraged him to face the forests and mountains of British Columbia as subject matter, bringing him into the mainstream of Canadian painting as represented by the Group of Seven. The National Gallery bought one of Macdonald's paintings in 1932; A. Y. Jackson was greatly impressed by his work; and in 1933 he became a founding member of the Canadian Group of Painters. But although Macdonald continued to paint representational landscapes throughout his career, he was also drawn to the Vancouver circle of artists and intellectuals who were interested in spiritualism.

Macdonald was impressed by the direction Lawren Harris's work was taking, and this, combined with his reading of P. D. Ouspensky's *Tertium Organum*, brought him to undertake a major re-evaluation of his own painting. In 1934 he began experimenting with the spiritual values of colour, responding to the theories of Wassily Kandinsky and Amédée Ozenfant, making semi-abstract pictures, the most substantial of which was *Formative Colour Activity* of 1934, which is now in the National Gallery. "The idiom," Macdonald wrote, "suggested flowers. . . . But I created the canvas with no preconceived planning. I drew nothing on the canvas. I just started off with pure vermilion."* This led to his first abstract paintings, works he initially called "thought expressions" and later "modalities." By the late 1930s he was making paintings similar to those of Lawren Harris—if less rigorously abstract—and when Harris moved to Vancouver in 1940, the two men became good friends, sharing studio space for a time.

Another influence and a further development in his abstract work came after 1943, when Grace Pailthorpe arrived in Vancouver. A physician, Freudian analyst, member of the British Surrealist movement, and painter, Pailthorpe urged Macdonald to paint more directly—intuitively rather than intellectually. Through the 1940s and early 1950s, he produced what he called "automatics," mostly small watercolours, freely and spontaneously created.

*Joyce Zemans, *Jock Macdonald: The Inner Landscape* (Toronto: Art Gallery of Ontario, 1981), p.54.

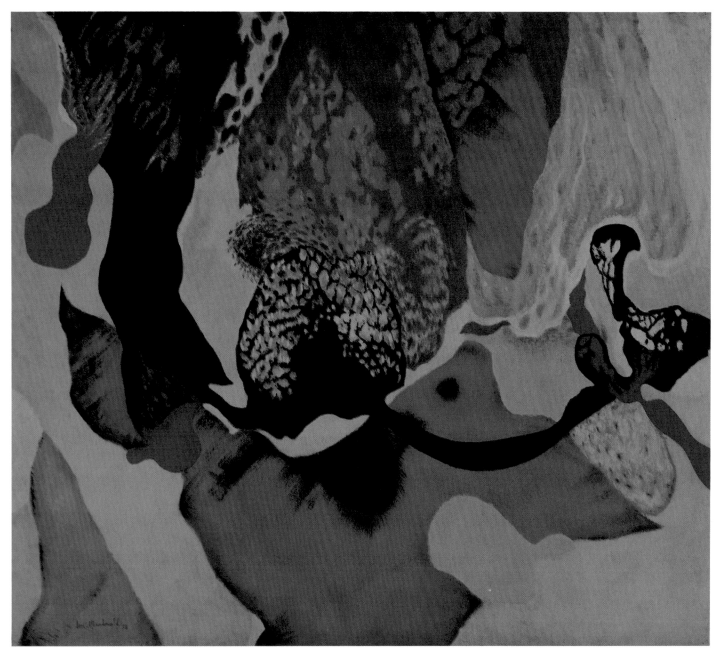

Jock Macdonald
Coral Fantasy (1958),
oil and lucite 44 on canvas, 106.4 × 122.0 cm.
Purchase, 1985.
Accession No. 28812.

In 1947, after a year teaching in Calgary, Macdonald moved to Toronto to take an appointment at the Ontario College of Art. Over the thirteen years he taught there, he gathered the deep respect of generations of students and fought lone, hard battles against the hidebound, regressive attitudes of many of his colleagues. He became a member of Painters Eleven at its formation in 1953. It was he who suggested to the American critic Clement Greenberg that he should visit Toronto, and Macdonald was encouraged by the criticism Greenberg gave of his work on his visit in 1957 (though his enthusiasm for the critic's support cooled later). In the last three years of his life, Macdonald made the strongest paintings of his career. He was working with broad, free gestures and on a larger scale than he had attempted before in his abstract pictures. It was as if all he had done in the previous decades was a preparation for this time.

The expressionistic character of these late paintings, like *Coral Fantasy* of 1958, opens them to a wide range of associations; their achievement is that they retain, first and last, the integrity of their own scale and space. The associations they suggest range from massive themes, such as mountain landscapes, to the minute worlds one can see only under a microscope. The notion of the bonding in all aspects of the universe, arising from Macdonald's interest in theosophic ideas, had been reflected in his earliest abstract works. It was a long struggle, however, to realize that rather than illustrating this unity in painting, he must parallel it by the independent integrity of painting itself. It was on this firm ground that the late paintings succeed. The title, *Coral Fantasy*, does not mean that the painting was *of* coral nor that the colouring, the pattern of forms, and the space they create suggested only a coral reef, but rather that the painting, like the coral reef, was its own world.

In the late 1950s, Macdonald was both excited by the direction his work was taking and gratified that the years of work and struggle were finally beginning to bring him public recognition. Even after his first heart attack in November 1960, he was soon back in his studio preparing to start work again, but early in December he was struck by a second and fatal seizure.

Jean Paul Lemieux

born 1904

The realization, in the early years of this century, of the values in "alternative" levels of art making—children's art, primitive art, folk art—has had a profound effect on the art of our times. Inevitably, there have been instances of exaggerated claims being made for minor "naive" achievements and unauthentic appropriations by "sophisticated" artists. It is a fine line that must be held by an artist whose conceptual approach and training is of the mainstream, yet who chooses to work in a naive style as the way of expressing his deep attachment to a place. It is the line that Jean Paul Lemieux has held since the 1930s in his paintings of the people and landscape of Quebec.

Lemieux's interest in Quebec's folk art and local histories was already well developed by his student days at the École des Beaux-Arts in Montreal. After a period of travel in France and the United States, he returned to Montreal to teach, first at the École des Beaux-Arts and then, in 1935, at the newly established École du Meuble. This school in Montreal had been set up by the Quebec government "to improve the quality of the crafts made and sold in Quebec, with one eye on tourism, as well as to provide a solution to rural poverty."* Despite its conservative purpose, the school became a centre of radical artistic thinking. (When Lemieux left in 1937 for the École des Beaux-Arts in Quebec, he was succeeded by Paul-Émile Borduas.) Lemieux's interest in Quebec folk art deepened during the 1930s, not only as a reflection on Quebec history and culture, but also as an expression of a society suffering harsh times under repressive conditions.

*Charles C. Hill, *Canadian Painting in the Thirties* (Ottawa: National Gallery, 1975), p.116.

Lemieux responded to the people, their customs and traditions, sometimes anecdotally, sometimes satirically, by painting in a manner that reflected his study of folk art, particularly of the Charlevoix district. Lemieux is best known, however, for his work since the 1950s, in which he has concentrated on figures isolated in landscape settings, such as *L'orpheline* of 1956. This painting is characteristic in its frontality and in the harshness of the portrayal, which emphasizes the pathos of the subject. The simple dress, the styleless hair, and the white bow mark the girl's attachment to institutional life, stressing her anonymity. Our first impression is that she is a type rather than an individual, yet Lemieux subtly causes us to recognize her as a person, if only by the way her mouth is set, by the curious twist of her upturned nose, and the way the light catches her eyes.

Lemieux set the course of his art as a conscious response to a place and its people, deliberately limiting his range. At the same time, he recognized that change to Quebec's isolation could only come from a broad awareness of its context. In an article he wrote in 1938 he came strongly to the defence of Alfred Pellan, who was being criticized for setting the measure of his work to international developments. Lemieux wrote: "Why should he be content with folklore images when he could go further? Why confine art within petty limits? Is not art universal?"**

**Ibid.*, p.132.

Jean Paul Lemieux
L'orpheline (1956),
oil on canvas, 60.9 × 45.6 cm.
Purchase, 1957.
Accession No. 6684.

Paul-Émile Borduas

1905–1960

In 1948, Paul-Émile Borduas published *Refus global*. This essay became a focal point in the conflict between the regressive conservatism that was intent on maintaining the political and intellectual status quo in Quebec, and the wide spectrum of opinion that sought change. In describing Québécois, it said:

> We are a small people sheltering under the wing of the clergy—the only remaining repository of faith, knowledge, truth, and national wealth; isolated from the universal progress of thought with all its pitfalls and perils, and raised (since complete ignorance was impossible) on well-meaning but grossly distorted accounts of the great historical facts.*

Ironically (but typically), Borduas's introduction to art came through the church. He grew up in Saint-Hilaire, the home of Ozias Leduc, and was fascinated by watching Leduc paint in the town's church. He apprenticed informally with Leduc, who in 1923 encouraged him to attend the recently opened École des Beaux-Arts in Montreal. In 1928, Leduc helped to arrange church support for Borduas to study at the Ateliers d'Art Sacré in Paris. Borduas returned to Canada in 1930 intending to work as a church painter, but with commissions then severely restricted, he made his living teaching drawing in the school system. A decisive change came in 1937 when he joined the faculty of the École du Meuble in Montreal and his eyes were opened to the range of advanced art. By the early 1940s he had gathered around him a group of students from the École du Meuble and the École des Beaux-Arts to discuss art theory and philosophy.

Borduas's own work developed hesitantly through the 1930s. Significant for him, as for other Quebec artists, was the exhibition that Alfred Pellan held after his return from Paris in 1940; it was a landmark exhibition in that it showed a Quebec artist whose work was directly in line with the most recent developments of Parisian art. Borduas's first major series of work in a new manner were some gouache-on-paper paintings he made in 1942, paintings with strong Surrealist overtones. Borduas was greatly influenced by André Breton and his Surrealist movement. Breton argued for a total revision of society by giving primacy to the resources of the unconscious in order to lead to a heightened spiritual and practical freedom.

Through the 1940s, Breton urged Borduas to join the international Surrealist movement. Borduas resisted this, partly because he felt that he and his small movement in Quebec would be swamped and partly because he felt that the situation in Quebec demanded an approach quite different from that faced by European artists. Borduas's group (which included Jean-Paul Riopelle, Fernand Leduc, Pierre Gauvreau, and Jean-Paul Mousseau) moved towards a Surrealist-based abstraction. Their first exhibition was held in 1946; but it was at their second exhibition, in 1947, that the critic Tancrède Marsil named them *Les Automatistes*, referring to the title of the key painting in that exhibition: Borduas's *Sous le vent de l'île*, which had the alternative title of *Automatisme 1.47*.

The image of *Sous le vent de l'île* was developed by the Surrealist method of free association. Pictorially, its essence lies in its development of a convincing, autonomous sense of space. The background, flatly and thinly painted, suggests a coastline seen from the air; the foreground consists of a series of floating forms, spreading indefinitely back into space. Borduas contrasts the two areas by the technique he employs to create an image of space. The background is brushed on in broad horizontal strokes; the foreground elements, running vertically, are laid on with a palette knife. The image retains naturalistic clues—a shoreline and, in the foreground, suggestions of leaves and apples. But as Borduas said of a similar composition, "Its subject is strictly subjective, and probably belongs to the still mysterious world of [private] associations."**

Borduas's cry, in *Refus global*, for spiritual and intellectual freedom roused powerful and intemperate opposition from the church and the government. Borduas maintained that this essay urged the individual to seek personal spiritual freedom, but in the climate of the times it was taken as a political polemic. The educational authorities felt that Borduas was exercising a corrupting influence on his students, and he was dismissed from his post at the École du Meuble. Although his prestige among advanced art circles grew in the succeeding years, he suffered intolerable personal and financial strain. In 1953 he left Montreal for the United States on what he intended to be an extended

*Ramsay Cook, ed., *French-Canadian Nationalism: An Anthology* (Toronto: Macmillan, 1969).

**François-Marc Gagnon, *Paul-Émile Borduas* (Montreal: Montreal Museum of Fine Arts, 1988), p.220.

Paul-Émile Borduas
Sous le vent de l'île (1947),
oil on canvas, 114.7 × 147.7 cm.
Purchase, 1953.
Accession No. 6098.

Paul-Émile Borduas
Les Arènes de Lutèce (1953),
oil on canvas, 81.3 × 106.7 cm.
Gift from the Douglas M. Duncan
Collection, 1970.
Accession No. 16449.

period of self-exile. He went to Provincetown, then on to New York, and in 1955 to Paris. He always thought he would return to Montreal—maintaining close contacts with friends and regularly sending back work for exhibition—but he died in Paris in 1960.

The painting *Les Arènes de Lutèce* was probably made in Provincetown and was one of the leading works in his first New York show, at the Passedoit Gallery in January 1954. In the title, Lutèce refers to the original Roman name for Paris. The painting emerges directly from works such as *Sous le vent de l'île*, before the impact of New York Abstract Expressionism affected his work. In structure, the painting, built around contrasting vertical and horizontal planes, is reminiscent of the earlier painting, but now the foreground and background are tightly intermeshed, and residual references to the naturalistic world have been eliminated in favour of a rigorous abstraction. As the critic Rodolphe de Repentigny wrote at the time, "This kind of painting reaches a degree of visual purity seldom seen in the history of art."

Borduas's stay in New York and his contact with advanced painting there—the work of Jackson Pollock, Franz Kline, Robert Motherwell, and so on—had a marked effect not only on his art but also, because of the new perspectives opened to him, on his feelings for the culture and society he had just left. He realized two vital points: first, that a statement made through

painting had to set its own terms and abide by them, rather than being representative of other ways of expressing ideas; second, that real change came about not by being enclosed within a situation but by being open to the broadest context. Thus, he came to see his artistic concerns as in the direct line of modernist painting in the fullest sense. This led, in the Paris years, to a series of extraordinary paintings, in many of which black and white predominated.

One small but telling change in the late works is Borduas's shift from evocative poetic titles to simple descriptions—*Radiant*, *Thaw*, *Pulsation*—or to titles that use the word "composition" with a designating number. The title of the National Gallery picture *3 + 4 + 1* is a descriptive reading of the painting's dynamics through the black areas. The "3" refers to the three large areas of black that mark the curve from top left to bottom right; the "4" refers to the group in the lower left that leads back across the picture to the "1" in the upper right corner. By means of this sweeping movement across and around the surface, every part of the surface is engaged, and the movement is accentuated by the flow of the white areas (with pink and grey-green intermixed) which curve across the diagonal from lower left to upper right. At first, it seems that the black areas lie *on* the white field; looking closer, we see that the white overlays the black. This spatial ambiguity is directly related to another level of tension: Do the areas of black resist the white, or are they in the process of being wholly concealed by the white? These visual tensions are directly related to Borduas's physical working of the surface as he spread and pushed the thickly layered paint, emphasizing the process through which the image was formed.

Paul-Émile Borduas
3 + 4 + 1 (1956),
oil on canvas, 199.8 × 250.0 cm.
Purchase, 1962.
Accession No. 9858.

Borduas confused many of his supporters when he left Montreal by turning on them to criticize their continuing attachment to Surrealist practices and Automatism. But he was trying to make them see, as he had seen, that the real challenge transcended that of any particular place. Perhaps his most telling statement was when he wrote to Claude Gauvreau in 1959, "I belonged to my village first and then my province. I considered myself French-Canadian, and after my first trip to Europe more Canadian than French, Canadian (merely Canadian, just like my [Anglophone] compatriots) in New York, and lately North American. From now on I hope to 'possess' the whole world."†

†*Borduas and America* (Vancouver: Vancouver Art Gallery, 1977), p.27.

Alfred Pellan

1906–1988

In the summer of 1940, the Musée du Québec held a retrospective exhibition of the paintings of Alfred Pellan. The occasion turned into a reception for a returning hero; Pellan had been fourteen years in Paris, and the work he brought back with him was a revelation to Quebec artists. Canadian artists had been going to Paris to study for more than fifty years, but it was still rare for them to become involved in the most contemporary developments. Here, in Pellan's work, was a Québécois in touch with the leading edge of Parisian art.

Four years earlier, Pellan had applied for a teaching position at the École des Beaux-Arts and been turned down for his modernity and criticized for his internationalism. Yet it was precisely his modernity that excited so much attention in 1940. At a later stage, when Quebec artists learned more directly about recent European art, they could place Pellan's work within a broader context and see how his styles had been forged from a synthesis of a variety of approaches of the leading Cubist and Surrealist painters. Pellan's interest in Surrealism was strengthened in the 1940s partly in response to the importance of Surrealism in advanced art in Montreal at that time. He was drawn to its imaginative and poetic potentials rather than to its theoretical underpinning or political implications.

As an artist, Pellan was independent by nature and little interested in collective approaches or political stances. However, because of his stature in the Montreal artistic community, he could not avoid being drawn into disputes. The disputes were not only in opposition to reactionary opinions but were within the modernist movement itself, above all with Borduas. In 1943, Borduas argued that Pellan had compromised himself and the modernist movement in Quebec when he accepted a job at the École des Beaux-Arts in Montreal; under its conservative director Charles Maillard, the École was a bastion of reactionary academicism. Maillard and Pellan were often in dispute, and matters came to a head in 1945, with the result that Maillard was forced to resign.

By his defeat of Maillard, Pellan took a leading position in the move for reform in the art schools. At the same time, he became the centre of opposition to Borduas among the modernists. He disagreed with Borduas's maintenance of control over the artistic expression of his students, and he disputed the special claims made for the Automatiste movement, asserting that he had been doing automatism (*i.e.*, valuing chance associations) long before Borduas. In 1948, Pellan and fourteen other Quebec artists formed a short-lived group, *Prisme d'yeux*, to stress the primacy of individual expression and to argue against the position taken by Borduas and the Automatistes.

Alfred Pellan
Sur la plage (1945),
oil on canvas, 207.7 × 167.6 cm.
Purchase, 1961.
Accession No. 9512.

146

Through the 1930s and 1940s, Pellan's work demonstrated a broad catalogue of styles, ranging from the representational to the abstract. In the mid-1940s, he began to develop certain themes that he was to build on extensively in subsequent years, as well as to establish a distinctive stylistic range. In *Sur la plage* of 1945 and *Floraison* of around 1956, the National Gallery owns two early, major examples of Pellan's mature work.

Sur la plage is an erotic dream, or perhaps more of a daydream, in which a man watching some girls sunbathing, fantasizes over their display of themselves. The sun beats down on him; the atmosphere becomes charged, delirious even, and he is transformed by his fantasies—his hair at the front sweeps up to form horns, turning him into a satyr. Pellan works up a feverish image, compressing the women between the man's head and the buildings. Every part of the picture is broken into hard-edged interlocking shapes, and rather than modelling the figures by tone or modulation of colour, he describes them three-dimensionally by complex linear patterns. The frenetic style of the picture and, for its time and place, the audacity of its subject, reaffirmed the shock that Pellan had first injected into Quebec art five years earlier.

The metamorphic relationship of human and animal life to the plant world had been a constant theme in Surrealism since the 1920s. It became one of Pellan's most favoured interests, and from it arose some of his most intensely coloured and richly textured pictures. In approach, *Floraison* is reminiscent of the work of Paul Klee, not so much in the style of drawing or the use of colour, but in the way of building a magic garden where plants and flowers take on individual characteristics and seem to exhibit human personalities. In this garden a variety of plants grow. They are brightly coloured and distinguished in shape but are flat—all except one, a sunflower that explodes with colour and texture beyond the dimensions of all the others and, in its blossoming, seems to be the source of light on which the others jealously depend.

At the end of 1952, Pellan resigned from the École des Beaux-Arts and went back to Paris. His three-year stay culminated in a major exhibition at the Musée National d'Art Moderne in 1955, a very significant mark of the extent to which Pellan was accepted among the modern masters. The National Gallery of Canada organized a retrospective of Pellan's work in 1960 and was among the galleries to host the 1972 retrospective organized jointly by the Montreal Museum of Fine Arts and the Musée du Québec. Pellan's work has also become widely known outside the museum and gallery context through commissions for murals and stained glass, as well as through his involvement in the design of a range of theatre productions.

Jean-Paul Riopelle

born 1923

The surfaces of Jean-Paul Riopelle's paintings have often been compared to stained glass and mosaic, while their images have been described in terms of landscape. Europeans have tended to assume that because of Riopelle's Canadian background, his paintings reflect vast open spaces, and indeed Canadians have claimed his contribution to the landscape tradition that has defined so much of the art in this country. Yet neither the "landscape" analogy nor the "stained glass and mosaic" are truly appropriate. Stained glass and mosaic are among the least open and gestural of techniques, whereas at every point of Riopelle's career, painterly and graphic gestures have been the core of his pictorial language; and the structure of his paintings has principally been directed not to the vastness of landscape but to an intimate view of nature.

By way of example, Riopelle pointed out how the great pictorial space of Monet's *Waterlilies* was based on a little pond in the garden at Giverny, with a railway passing beside it. Of his own work he said, "I am not a painter of virgin forests, or prairies stretching to infinity." He said that everything needed to develop pictorial space could be found in the single leaf of a tree.* The essence lay in seeking to understand nature through the free gesture.

While a student at the École des Beaux-Arts in Montreal, Riopelle had joined the group of young artists associated with Borduas. As one of the Automatistes, he signed *Refus global* in 1948, and he designed the cover for the pamphlet. From 1945, however, he spent little time in Montreal. In that year he went to New York, and in 1946 he moved to Paris. He became a link between the Automatistes in Canada and the Surrealist movement in Paris, but disagreed with Borduas over the direction of the Canadian movement and its relationship to international Surrealism. As Riopelle became absorbed in the Parisian art scene and as his perspective broadened, he gradually withdrew from the concerns that engaged advanced art in Montreal.

*Pierre Schneider, *Riopelle: Signes mêlés* (Montreal: Leméac éditeur, 1972), pp.39–40.

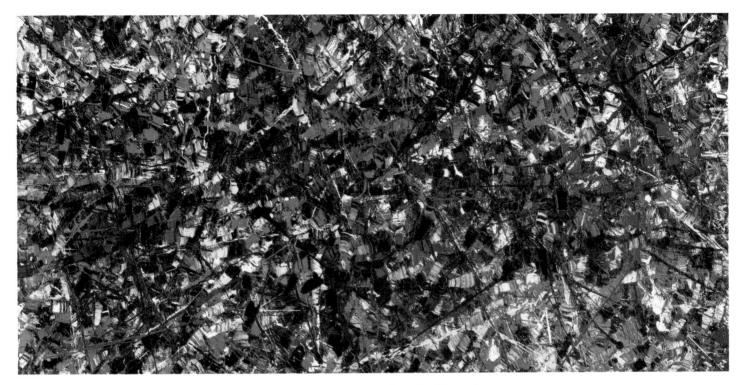

Jean-Paul Riopelle
Knight Watch (1953),
oil on canvas, 96.6 × 194.8 cm.
Purchase, 1954.
Accession No. 6253.

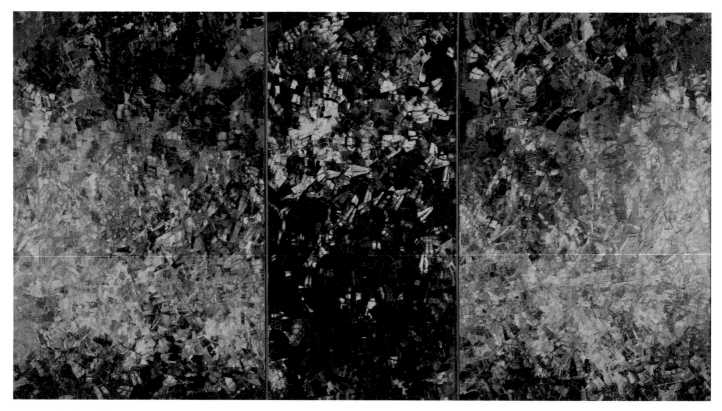

Jean-Paul Riopelle
Pavane (1954),
oil on canvas, 300.0 × 550.2 cm assembled;
triptych, centre panel, 300.0 × 149.7 cm, side panels,
300.0 × 200.2 cm.
Purchase, 1963.
Accession No. 15038.

By the mid-1940s, in paintings and watercolours, Riopelle was pushing towards a radical pictorial structure—breaking down the figure-ground description of space for an "all-over" surface based on the primacy of the gesture. By 1947, he was experimenting in withdrawing the distinction between the colour areas and the linear elements by using thinners over the colours to make the paint drip down the canvas. The linear elements thus arose out of the colour taches rather than being separate graphic gestures ("tache," which means a dot or blob, in this context becomes the basic pictorial building block, a gesture made with a brush or palette knife). Riopelle extended this approach in the paintings of the very early 1950s by dripping and weaving skeins of paint among the thick taches of colour that covered the canvases. This structure was fully developed by 1953, as we see in *Knight Watch*. Here, closely linked layers of rich colour applied with a palette knife and brush are combined with linear strokes and dribbles of paint that spread in all directions across the picture, binding and energizing the surface.

The paintings of the following year, 1954, saw another step in the development of Riopelle's pictorial structure, a step brilliantly exemplified by the massive *Pavane*, a triptych some three metres high and more than five metres across. Now the linear skeins have gone and the painting is composed of an incredibly complex multi-layered structure of palette knife strokes.

Sometimes these strokes are of single colours, but often each stroke contains several distinct colours. Although certain colours predominate in particular areas, the viewer's perception of colour in the picture is broadened by the optical mixing of colours to produce an overall effect of dynamic brilliance. The linear and colour qualities of the painting are now wholly combined within the same pictorial element, within each distinct stroke of the palette knife.

The title *Pavane* refers to a Spanish dance that originated in the sixteenth century. The dance was one of slow, courtly elegance, with the participants richly costumed, its name possibly referring to the display of the peacock. The music for the dance was based on a two-beat bar. The two outer sections of *Pavane* are equal in size, similar in colour range and form. The narrower central section breaks that symmetry, imposing a dark pause against the whites, while gathering in its upper part the same red that appears in the outer corners of the picture. Riopelle plays against the expectations of compositional harmony, of balance between line and colour, light and dark, and yet casts everything into a unified structure, a structure built up from the small palette knife gestures. As he said of the single leaf, "It is the whole forest. Everything can be seen there."

Jack Bush

1909–1977

In the late 1960s and early 1970s, Jack Bush's work came to represent the polarization of opinion over Canadian cultural identity. On one side were those people who saw Bush as a clear example of "selling-out" to American cultural infiltration; on the other were those who saw in Bush the model of a Canadian artist who was challenging the cultural mainstream and was succeeding. In the twenty years since then, with increasing numbers of Canadian artists exhibiting abroad, it has become clear that art in Canada has gained immeasurably in strength by taking up the challenge of joining the international scene. Ironically, in this same period, the tide of fashion has turned against the abstract colour-field painting that Bush practised.

Bush made no excuses for the direction he came to take nor for the ambition he harboured. He described it in terms of the difference between major and minor leagues: "If you've got enough nerve and are good enough, you can play in the majors."* But it was a long and gradual process for him. For the first twenty-five years of his career he worked closely within the current mode of Toronto art, which remained dominated by the Group of Seven and their successors in the Canadian Group of Painters. The change came in the 1950s with the formation of Painters Eleven, of which Bush was a member, and with their determination to look beyond provincial boundaries. The turning point for Bush himself came with the visit to Toronto in 1957 of the American critic Clement Greenberg. Of the artists Greenberg spoke with, Bush was the one who was most influenced by his advice. The two men became good friends.

In essential respects, however, Bush never denied the early origins of his work or the personality of his painterly expression. Although in the early 1960s he was deeply impressed by the work of younger American artists such as Frank Stella and Kenneth Noland, his painting never followed their systematic re-evaluation of painting's basic premises. In this respect, he remained closer to an older generation of American artists—Robert Motherwell and Adolph Gottlieb, for instance—and their response to the tradition of European painting.

This is apparent even in the mid-1960s, when Bush was making paintings such as *Tall Spread*, which in their formalism and colour-abstraction come closest to the contemporary work of the younger American painters.

**Jack Bush: A Retrospective* (Toronto: Art Gallery of Ontario, 1976).

Unlike the Americans' systematic pictorial structures, Bush's approach remained intuitive; and despite the abstractness of the paintings, his pictures remained image-oriented in the traditional sense of the visual tension between figure and ground. His paintings can be grouped into types, such as "Thrusts," "Sashes," "Columns," "Banners," and so on, which identify their formal appearance as well as linking them into our broader experience. Many of his paintings in the 1970s refer in their titles to music and in image to colour notes that he set in swinging sequences across coloured grounds.

In the mid-1960s Bush was making paintings in which stacks of colours were set in the centre of the painting and were enclosed on either side by areas of a single hue. He then began to move the colour stack to one side, so that in *Tall Spread* it fills three-quarters of the painting, bound or ordered by the vertical single-colour stripe on the left. The structure retains the figure-ground ambiguity: Do we read the stack as coming forward from a ground, or do we see the vertical stripe as being simply another colour on the same plane as the colours in the stack? The bands of the stack alternate in tone between dark and light, but the colours are grouped not according to a logical sequence but in an intuitive play from one to the next—a complex play, which in the end not only convinces us that the stack can "stand up" but impresses us with its monumentality, with its height one-and-a-half times human scale. Even then, it is not a rigid mechanical structure; it is one that seems to be in the process of being built, because of its "hand-made" character: the colours in the stack vary in width, their edges do not fall precisely parallel to one another, and the transition between one colour and another is soft, as if one colour might flow into another.

The character of *Tall Spread*, like the character of Bush's work as a whole, remains emphatically expressive. Its abstract form asserts its independence as a painting—an object distinct from other objects—but its play of shapes and colours, its "hand-made" character, and its scale reflect human measure.

Jack Bush
Tall Spread (1966),
acrylic on canvas, 271.0 × 127.1 cm.
Purchase, 1966.
Accession No. 14974.

Harold Town

born 1924

We cannot prepare ourselves for the way that one series of Harold Town's work follows another. We can anticipate its inventiveness, and we can be certain of its quality, but we can assume nothing about its subject, its style, or its technique. The course of Town's work has been full of surprises. The only certain pattern is his extraordinarily creative capacity and his command of the technical means that give it expression.

Town's prodigious output has, for the most part, comprised a succession of themes around which he plays variations. A theme may emerge as his response to any number of things. It may come from a particular technique or medium, as with the *Single Autographic Prints*, the *Snaps*, and the *Stages*. It may come from his attraction to a particular object or image; this was how the *Vale Variations* and the *Toy Horses* came into being. Or it may come from a particular class of images, such as the photographs that are the basis of the *Film Stars*, the *Famous* drawings, and the *Musclemen* paintings. The extent of a series varies considerably—some occupied him for a relatively short time, while others were developed over several years, comprising hundreds of individual works.

The *Single Autographic Prints* was his first fully developed series. Each is a monoprint, a unique work. The very techniques by which these prints were formed ruled out the possibility of making multiple impressions. Town began to make the prints in December 1953 and stopped abruptly five years later.

This period coincided with the existence of the Painters Eleven group to which he belonged. The prints were made on a Bavarian limestone and printed on a lithographic press. The early ones were principally linear images printed in one or two colours. As the series progressed, Town continually tested and expanded the range of the technique, rejecting traditional approaches. He started to use multiple inkings and to develop the images not only by conventional drawing but by printing from many different materials: cut-outs from paper, "found" shapes in cardboard, lengths of string, and pieces of leather and felt. In some cases, he collaged materials onto the prints.

Within the *Single Autographic Prints* there are several subgroups; for example, there is one that reflects Town's admiration of Oriental art and poetry, another that refers to classical mythology, and another referring to historical figures and events. *The First Aeroplane* can be grouped with a number of prints that seem to record the achievements of an eccentric inventor, prints such as *The First Infernal Submarine, Radar Detecting Winter*, and *Radar Detecting Spring. The First Aeroplane* is built up from several layers of colour and is shaped from a variety of materials. The result is a surface of extraordinary texture, and a sense of space suggested by the complex colour atmosphere that arises from the transparency in the layers of printing inks.

Harold Town
The First Aeroplane (1956),
autographic print on wove paper, 63.7 × 48.4 cm plate,
50.0 × 40.0 cm.
Purchase, 1957.
Accession No. 6872.

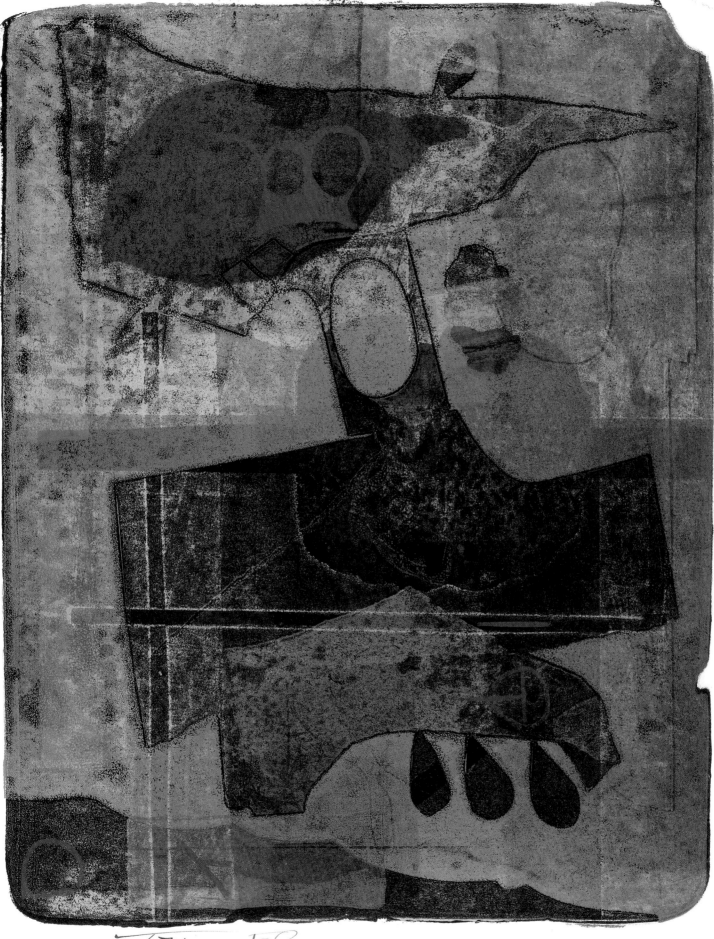

155

The *Single Autographic Prints* extended the range and definition of printmaking, and Town's achievements were widely recognized by the attention these works received in major international exhibitions. The very processes he was using, layering inks and applying materials, were in effect a form of collage of which the print was an impression. From 1957 on, he began to divide his time between the prints and collages. Over the following three years he made a group of large collages, often, as with *Music Behind*, on plywood supports.

Collage in art, both as technique and as a way to develop images, has a history of dissent. Its introduction by Braque and Picasso challenged the conventions of painting; its use by the German artist Kurt Schwitters was a radical comment on his times as he made art from objects that people discard: tickets, newspapers, packages, and so on. An aspect of dissent is, I think, apparent in Town's early use of collage. Until then, it had played essentially no part in Canadian art; his use of it stood as a challenge to the tradition of art around him. It was also an assertion of independence from the hold that Abstract Expressionism had on advanced art of that time, an assertion made piquant by the fact that the American critic Clement Greenberg (whom Town had refused to meet on his visit to Toronto) published an article in 1957 broadly dismissing recent developments in collage.

Above all, Town's interest in collage is as instinctive as his need to draw. Just as instinctive is the challenge he sets himself by working with two such opposed methods: drawing based on reduction and abstraction, and collage as the process of gathering in, accumulating, reforming, and re-presenting fragments from our object-ridden world.

Music Behind is one of the finest of these collages of the 1950s: complex, multilayered, and full of humour and ambiguous allusions. Onto the plywood support, Town glued the back panel from a television set. In the upper part, he inserted drinking straws into the perforations, and he glued other straws flat to the surface. He poured paint down the surface so that it was filtered and guided by the straws. Other elements are affixed—a fan, bottle labels, a domed plastic cover, and a razor blade that looks like a lobster claw. Around the central section the surface is covered with layers of tissue paper, and through them we can identify other elements: sheets of music and other printed matter. The whole effect is a witty play, combining Cubist collage techniques with the drip-and-splatter methods of American Abstract Expressionist painting. The character of *Music Behind*, as of all Town's collages, is that it makes a strong, overall formal statement and, as we move closer to it, that it engages us with a multitude of funny and intriguing details. It is so much a part of his art—generous and inventive, independent and peerless.

Harold Town
Music Behind (1958–59),
collage of masonite T.V. back panel with plastic component, cardboard container, straws, labels, stamps and envelope, music sheets, fan, razor blade, thread, fabric, string, arborite, corrugated cardboard, printed papers, tissue paper, and gouache on masonite, 103.2 × 102.5 cm.
Purchase, 1985.
Accession No. 28701.

William Ronald

born 1926

Jock Macdonald, writing to Alexandra Luke in 1955, noted, "It was a pity Ronald had gone—he won't return from New York I am sure—a very big error to do so."* William Ronald had left Toronto for New York the previous year, convinced that he had to meet the challenge of that city directly. Yet he had already made an important contribution to developing an active advanced-art scene in Toronto. In conjunction with Carrie Cardell, an interior decorator at the Robert Simpson Company, he had taken up an idea that had worked successfully in New York and had developed the "Abstracts at Home" exhibition in October 1953. In this exhibition, Ronald's work and that of six other artists— Jack Bush, Alexandra Luke, Oscar Cahén, Ray Mead, Kazuo Nakamura, and Tom Hodgson—was shown in room and window displays at Simpsons.

Subsequently, these artists decided to group together to find further ways of exhibiting, and with the addition of Jock Macdonald, Harold Town, Walter Yarwood, and Hortense Gordon, they formed Painters Eleven. Ronald maintained his contacts with the group after his move to New York. But his efforts to involve the group more closely with the activity in New York— including his part in getting Clement Greenberg to visit Toronto—were controversial and far-reaching in their implications. He cut his ties with Painters Eleven in 1957; and in 1963, two years before he returned to Canada, he took out United States citizenship. For six years he showed, with considerable success, at the Kootz Gallery, which was one of the leading venues of new art in New York.

Ronald's paintings of the earlier 1950s reflected the "all-over" gestural surfaces that marked the work of Jackson Pollock, Willem de Kooning, and Bradley

Walker Tomlin. By the mid-fifties, he was reacting against this with the development of his "central-image" pictures, such as *The Hero* of 1957. His approach had been one of attack since his earliest works; now, giving regard to the painterly structure advocated by Hans Hofmann, the attack was set towards surfaces activated by the tensions set up between one area and another, between drawing and colour, surface and illusion.

The image for *The Hero* came from a black-and-white movie poster of George Raft; the title carries the mythic overtones characteristic of so much Abstract Expressionist painting. Barnett Newman described this as a need to reassert man's natural desire for the exalted: "[By] making *cathedrals* out of Christ, man, or 'life,' we are making them out of ourselves, out of our own feelings. The image we produce is the self-evident one of revelation, real and concrete, that can be understood by anyone who will look at it without the nostalgic glasses of history."**

The sense of the real and the concrete of Ronald's *Hero* lies in the autonomy of the artistic structure, generated from the centre, reaching and engaging the dimensions of the picture. The image is one of presence, detached and imposing, yet also of flesh and blood with a human vulnerability marked in the tentative set of the head on a neck that seems barely capable of supporting it. This image of expressive presence gained a specific reference more than twenty years later in Ronald's freely interpretive portrait of Pierre Trudeau, the central painting of his ambitious series, *The Prime Ministers of Canada*.

*Joan Murray, *Painters Eleven in Retrospect* (Oshawa: Robert McLaughlin Gallery, 1979), p.16.

**"The Sublime Is Now," *The Tiger's Eye*, No.6, Dec.1948, p.51.

William Ronald
The Hero (1957),
oil on canvas, 183.0 × 183.0 cm.
Purchase, 1985.
Accession No. 28768.

Jack Shadbolt

born 1909

One of the ironic consequences of the Group of Seven's aspirations for an art of national identity was that, in the final result, it became a limiting form of regionalism. As such, it perpetuated an idea rather than nurturing a development. There were two related but distinct problems: first, a national scale in Canadian art before the Second World War still meant a small number of artists and a limited range of work; second, small though the scene was, the vast scale of the country and the particular developments within it gave great emphasis to the regions as social and cultural entities. This was nowhere more important than on the West Coast where, from the late 1920s, a small but identifiable artistic scene existed, shaped by a sense of isolation and by the extraordinary richness of the natural surroundings.

The reality of what regionalism means in its most vital form can be no better exemplified than by the career and work of Jack Shadbolt, who for some sixty years has been a major force as a painter and teacher. Moreover, the reality of regionalism to Shadbolt was the result not of an unknowing limitation but of decisions he made in the light of other options. After graduating from the Vancouver School of Art, he travelled and studied in New York, London, and Paris through the course of the 1930s. He enlisted in the army in 1942, hoping to join the War Art Program. He was posted to England in 1944, but rather than being sent into the field as he had hoped, he remained in London as an administrative officer. During this period, his interest in Surrealism led him to a way of understanding abstraction as he studied photographs of bomb destruction in Europe and observed the evidence of such destruction in London. Years afterwards he wrote about how "you get a memory image of what was there [after a building had been destroyed] but vastly altered and psychologically made infinitely more intense than the original thing."* Later, he linked this vision to the "X-ray" images in Indian art that had for so long impressed him.

*Jack Shadbolt: Early Watercolours (Victoria: Art Gallery of Greater Victoria, 1980), p.8.

Shadbolt came to recognize that he could make the most meaningful contribution in his own work if, instead of becoming a part of the international movement (as he might have done), he applied his experience of the outside world to his own immediate context. Only by such an approach could regionalism be regenerated and remain open to development.

Shadbolt's work interprets at many levels the richness of the West Coast. His approach has been less in terms of conventional landscape than in abstracting elements from nature; or, as in *Winter Theme No. 7* of 1961 (National Gallery), by using an initial image (here of boats) as the starting point for a process of formal transformation—from boats to beetles and seed pods.

The sense of natural growth and the cyclical forces of nature have always played a central role in Shadbolt's work, linking up with his great respect for the art of the Northwest Coast Indians and the way in which a spiritual life—in legend and in reality—inhabits the coastal landscape. *Presences after Fire*, a watercolour made in 1950, shows this amalgamation. In this painting, Shadbolt's knowledge and appreciation of developments such as Cubism and Surrealism are united with his sense of the spirit in the landscape, represented here by spectral figures surviving after the destruction of the forest.

Jack Shadbolt
Presences after Fire (1950),
watercolour and gouache with pen and black ink on wove
paper, 68.5 × 93.5 cm.
Purchase, 1953.
Accession No. 6112.

Ronald Bloore

born 1925

In 1958, Ronald Bloore, a painter and art historian, was appointed director of the Norman Mackenzie Art Gallery in Regina, Saskatchewan. The gallery had opened five years earlier as part of Regina College. Bloore stayed there seven years before returning to Toronto. An active advanced-art scene had already begun to develop in the city, made unique by the Emma Lake Workshops. These workshops had been initiated in 1955 by Kenneth Lochhead, director of the art school at Regina College, to give professional artists the opportunity to work under the leadership of a major figure. Jack Shadbolt, Joe Plaskett, and Will Barnet had led the first three workshops. In 1959 Barnett Newman, one of the leaders of advanced painting in New York, was invited to Emma Lake. His visit had a major effect on the development of the workshops, proving that remoteness of location and a limited tradition were not a bar to meeting the challenge of advanced international art. On an individual level, Newman's presence and example were a great encouragement to the artists who attended the workshops, as Bloore, among others, has attested.

The following year, Bloore organized an exhibition at the Norman Mackenzie to show the work of five Regina painters—Lochhead, Art McKay, Ted Godwin, Doug Morton, and himself—and an architect, Clifford Wiens. This exhibition, minus Wiens's contributions, was circulated by the National Gallery as "Five Painters from Regina." It brought these artists to national attention and showed that, in awareness and quality, their work was as challenging as that being done anywhere in the country.

The Regina Five were a group because of where they lived and because of the experimentation of their work, but not by adherence to a common program. Such a notion would have been unthinkable to Bloore who, for more than thirty years, has pursued a rigorous and personal direction. In his catalogue statement for the "Five Painters from Regina," he wrote: "I am not aware of any intention while painting with the exception of making a preconceived image function formally as a painting. By this I mean that the appearance of each work has been consciously determined in my mind before executing it, and the general concept is not significantly altered by the requirements of material limitations."

This was striking at two levels, particularly in the context of the time. First, the idea of beginning with a "preconceived image" went against the current notion of intuitive expression. Second, for most abstract painters, the activity of painting was a determining factor in the outcome of a work. Bloore's position is underscored by his repeated contention that nothing new in painting has been achieved since Cimabue, the great master of the Italian thirteenth century, in the sense that all the essential issues about painting as such had been formulated by that time.

Bloore set rigorous parameters within which to work: a surely constructed abstraction limited in colour—white, blue, red, but above all, white—and using with it a simple range of geometric forms. Many of his paintings comprise only linear forms; others include stars, circles, arches, or triangles, forms he has described as "symbol-like elements," not because he proposes specific meaning by them but because they are forms deeply embedded in the history of art. In structural terms, he has been greatly influenced by architectural forms, particularly those of ancient civilizations, whose currency has never been devalued.

White Line No. 2 was made in 1962, a white-in-white painting whose shapes and textures seem both to create light and to symbolize it. There is a dual symmetry to the painting, one composed of verticals and horizontals moving towards the centre of the picture, the other where there is a shift in rhythm at the centre, which forms a circle. The interlocking of these two structures is like a source of light; everything is of the same order, but the centre appears visually magnified and intensified.

Ronald Bloore
White Line No. 2 (1962),
oil on masonite, 121.5 × 198.8 cm.
Purchase, 1984.
Accession No. 28502.

Gershon Iskowitz

1921–1988

Gershon Iskowitz's work is a monument to the triumph of the spirit over evil and the transcendence of horror by the joy that is expressible through painting.

Iskowitz was born and brought up in the Polish city of Kielce. From childhood his central interest was in drawing and painting, and in the fall of 1939 he was set to begin studies at the Warsaw Academy of Art. Kielce was bombarded and then entered by the Germans on 3 September. Iskowitz was pressed into forced labour for the next four years. In 1942 all his immediate family, with the exception of one of his brothers, were among the eighteen thousand Jews from Kielce who were taken for "resettlement." Transported to Treblinka, they were subsequently murdered. The following year, Iskowitz and his brother were sent to Auschwitz. There they were separated, and his brother was later killed. In 1944, Iskowitz was moved once again, this time to Buchenwald.

Near the end of the war, hearing stories that SS squads were killing concentration camp prisoners to prevent them from being liberated, Iskowitz attempted to escape while out on a working party. He was shot and left for dead. Fellow prisoners later carried him back to the camp, and he was among the small number of survivors freed from Buchenwald by American troops in April 1945. Iskowitz spent the next four years in Munich, the first two in hospital. He began to paint again, studied briefly at the Munich Academy of Art, and received private lessons from Oskar Kokoschka. In 1949, sponsored by an uncle who lived in Toronto, he immigrated to Canada, bringing with him three wartime drawings that he had been able to save, two of them made while in Buchenwald.

The transition to life in Canada—culturally, materially, and psychologically—was tough and painful, and all the more so because of his determination to be an artist. He earned some money making portraits, but much of his work was private, consumed with his wartime experiences, with memories of his family, and with the chance of circumstances that had allowed him to survive. Gradually he gained the confidence to look outwards. He began to make expeditions into the countryside north of Toronto to draw and paint, later extending his trips up into the Parry Sound region. The paintings and watercolours he made were, from the start, free impressions of the landscape, and by the mid-1960s the literal references to the landscape had all but disappeared in favour of expressive abstractions of light and colour.

A turning point in the development of his painting came in 1967 when, with the aid of a Canada Council grant, Iskowitz went to northern Manitoba and flew by helicopter in the area around Churchill. Through the experience of flying close to the ground, of climbing and diving, he had the sensation of being immersed in the dynamic patterns of changing colours and forms—from trees to lakes, hills to valleys. "I saw," he said, "all those things that were happening in my paintings." The effect on his work was immediate and striking. He heightened the key of his colour, began to work with the textures and transparent qualities of his paint, and became eager to expand the scale of his pictures.

Two major series, the *Lowlands* and *Uplands*, developed directly from his helicopter flying. The *Lowlands* reflect the action of diving to the ground; the *Uplands*, to the view as the aircraft pulled up over the trees and hills. He made eleven paintings in the *Uplands* group between 1969 and 1972. The first, *Triptych*, was followed by ten paintings in diptych form, *Uplands A* to *Uplands K* (the letter "I" was omitted). The series formed the core of the paintings selected when Iskowitz represented Canada at the Venice Biennale in 1972.

As with all the paintings in the group, *Uplands E* combines two viewpoints: the background is lighter in hue and is divided horizontally, as if between the earth and sky. In front of this, a large irregular mass appears to hover. This form, reflecting the sensation of movement above the trees, is more densely painted and is made up in layer on layer of irregular colour patches, some partially concealed within the mass, others bursting brilliantly through. Iskowitz described his work as the desire to express the experience of being immersed in light and colour. His legacy is a unique interpretation of landscape, which expresses his joy and freedom in painterly creation and which for us, as spectators, is both astonishing and humbling.

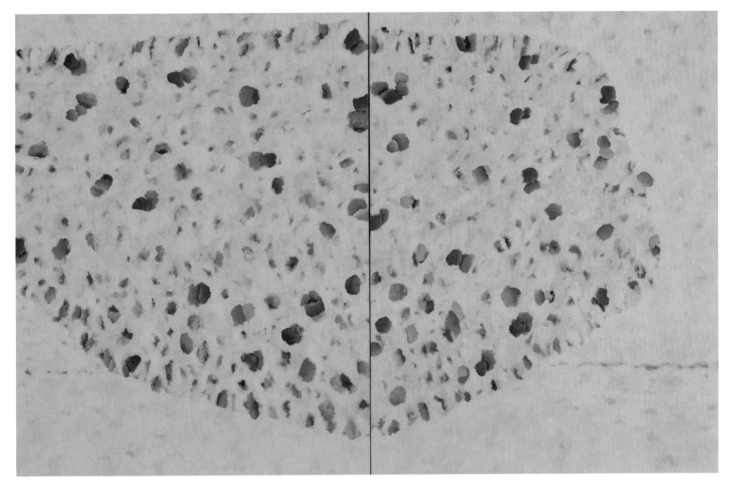

Gershon Iskowitz
Uplands E (1971),
acrylic on canvas, 228.6 × 356.0 cm overall;
two panels, 228.6 × 178.0 cm each.
Purchase, 1972.
Accession No. 16993.

William Kurelek

1927–1977

The tent is pitched close to the forest edge; it is almost a part of the forest, with its tall poles and its spreading canopy making a broad and generous welcome. Inside, tables are piled high with food, and planks of wood supported by chairs are ready to serve as seating. Final touches to the arrangements are being made, and steins of beer are being drawn even as the first guests begin to take their places. A flat-footed country band flavours the sense of occasion. Whether roused by the rhythm of the band or simply in anticipation of the feast, a group of children are causing mayhem. Elsewhere, family groups, with the awkwardness of those unused to formality, await their turn to be greeted by their hosts.

The high viewpoint of the picture *Manitoba Party*, with its wide angle on the proceedings, embraces a multiplicity of incident. But it distances as well, setting it out like a map of memories. William Kurelek, who made the picture in 1964, recalled in it two parties given by neighbours during the years that he lived with his family on a farm at Stonewall, Manitoba. The Kureleks had moved there from Whitford, Alberta, where William had been born. So much in Kurelek's work took its subject and meaning from his childhood on prairie farms through the harsh years of the Depression. So much also came from the complex and often distressing relationship with his father, who did not appreciate his son's artistic interests until many years later.

Kurelek had decided that he wanted to paint when he was very young. In his twenties, he sought a discipline of training, attending art schools in Toronto, Mexico, and England, but leaving each time in disappointment. While in England he also sought relief for his chronic depression, and for a number of years he was under psychiatric care. Part of his treatment at the Netherne Psychiatric Hospital involved participation in a progressive art therapy program through which he produced works of dark and compelling strength. He had much earlier rejected the Greek Orthodox faith of his Ukrainian background, and after years of spiritual emptiness he converted in 1957 to Roman Catholicism, realizing the purpose of his work as being to express his religious convictions. Much of his best painting is concerned explicitly or implicitly with Christian themes, invariably brought into a modern context and often linked to situations in the rural life he had known as a child. He saw himself as working within a specific tradition: "Consider the works of the great propagandists, moralisers, illustrators—Bosch's and Bruegel's religious and social satire. . . . Goya's *Horrors of War* etchings; Hogarth's *The Rake's Progress* paintings; Daumier's political satire cartoons; even Diego Rivera's communist murals. . . . I have something to say, just as they did."* Working within this tradition meant bringing the universal themes to the specific reference of his own life—his upbringing in the West, his working life in Toronto, his record of travels across Canada.

Kurelek returned to Canada from England in 1959 and held his first one-man exhibition the following year at the Isaacs Gallery in Toronto. Over the next seventeen years he painted prolifically and exhibited widely and frequently. He also spread knowledge of his work through many illustrated books and through his autobiography, *Someone with Me*. He deliberately sought popularity with his work, producing what he called his "pot boilers," not only as a means of supporting his family but also to draw attention to what he considered his major works, his moralizing religious pictures. Inevitably, there is an uneven quality in his output; but many pictures, in both the "moralizing" and "story-telling" categories, are striking in their vision, direct and sensitive in their observations of people. There are funny paintings and sad ones, distressing paintings and joyous ones. Painting was the way Kurelek knew to exorcize his demons, to express his sincerest convictions, and to draw others into sharing his experience.

*Joan Murray, *Kurelek's Vision of Canada* (Oshawa: Robert McLaughlin Gallery, 1982), p.71.

William Kurelek
Manitoba Party (1964),
oil on masonite, 121.9 × 152.6 cm.
Purchase, 1965.
Accession No. 14761.

Alex Colville

born 1920

The subjects of Alex Colville's pictures are almost invariably concerned with two distinct but co-existent worlds: the world of human beings and the world of animals. (Since 1950, he has made only two compositions without human or animal subjects—*Snowstorm* and *Elm Tree at Horton Landing*.) In the pictures in which both humans and animals appear, each is secure in the other's presence, but the atmosphere of interdependence also reveals the unbridgeable gap between them. Colville has often spoken about the innocence of animals, the innocence that reciprocates their complete absorption in their own world. "The idea of a bad dog," he has said, "is absolutely inconceivable to me, unless it has been driven crazy by people." People, who are both endowed with and burdened with consciousness and will, capable of reflecting on the lives they lead and recognizing the passage of past and present to future, can lead lives for evil or for good.

The painting *Hound in Field* is one of Colville's most felicitous. It captures fully and unerringly the animal's engagement with its world, the indivisibility between its existence and its environment. This indivisibility is expressed in the beauty of unity between the dog— alert, focused, asymmetrical and yet perfectly balanced—and its surroundings.

Since the early 1950s, Colville has developed his compositions on the basis of complex geometric schemes. Every aspect and detail of a composition is carefully measured and proportioned for the place it occupies in the whole. *Hound in Field* is a rare exception to this rule. Colville made no geometric drawings for it, and he has said that the composition and balance of the picture came out "like magic." Yet the underlying structure exists. The painter Christopher Pratt studied the picture very closely and realized that the positioning and shaping of the dog exactly described a "whirling circle," a spiral figure developed from a golden section. The golden section is a mathematical ratio discovered by the Greeks in the fifth century BC. Called the "divine proportion," it has had immense importance in the theory and practice of art and architecture.

Alex Colville
Hound in Field (1958),
casein tempera on masonite, 76.3 × 101.5 cm.
Purchase, 1959.
Accession No. 7163.

Alex Colville
To Prince Edward Island (1965),
acrylic emulsion on masonite, 61.9 × 92.5 cm.
Purchase, 1966.
Accession No. 14954.

The sense of absorption that marks *Hound in Field*, the animal's indifference to our observing presence, is very different from the confrontation in the 1965 painting, *To Prince Edward Island*. Colville's compositions are often developed by combining two distinct ideas or experiences. The process of uniting them is frequently extended over a period of years. In this case, he was fascinated by the image of two figures, a man and a woman, with one of them looking through binoculars.

"Why was I intrigued?" he has said. "I don't know; just that there was *something* I sensed in it. It had some *meaning*." In 1960 he made a rough sketch with a woman using binoculars, her elbows resting on a window sill, and a man beside her with his back to the window. Colville took up the idea again in 1963 and once more abandoned it. Then, "after a trip to Prince Edward Island in 1965 I suddenly realized that I was going to be able to work with two people and the binoculars—that the boat would do it."*

*David Burnett, *Colville* (Toronto: McClelland and Stewart, 1983), p.222.

The man sits relaxed. He appears content to be carried along by the vessel. But the woman, who had been facing him, has twisted around in her seat, intent on the view through the binoculars, her index finger resting on the focusing ring. In contrast to the unity of the animal with its environment in *Hound in Field*, *To Prince Edward Island* reveals the self-awareness of people, but in two contrasting ways: the man in an attitude of acceptance, the woman in one of acute scrutiny. Colville's initial fascination with the idea was realized by how "the boat would do it"—how the contrasting viewpoints could be focused on "meaning" by the link with the traditional symbol of the vessel as the passage of life and the sea as eternity.

Christopher Pratt

born 1935

In discussing his austere and symmetrical painting *House in August*, 1969 (Collection of Mr. and Mrs. William Teron), Christopher Pratt said that it gave "a sense of a kind of person, a sense of a kind of place, a sense of a kind of situation. . . . I get a sense of myself."* This describes so much of the tension in Pratt's work. His art is always precise and measured, and his images consist of only a few elements, each of which is reduced to a typical form. Yet as he says, it is a *sense* that arises out of the image rather than an inventory of facts, a sense that may lie in the pleasure gained from a formal structure perfectly balanced, or the sense of facing a situation of uncertainty, a condition filled with anxiety.

The image of the house, in both literature and art, has long been taken as a symbol of the human body and a metaphor for psychological conditions. It is an image that Pratt has painted time and again, originating in his memories of wood-clad houses on the rocky Newfoundland coast and distilled into a geometrically precise structure isolated beside a sea of idyllic calm and blueness. In the interior views, the house will sometimes be inhabited, usually by a female figure; but more often it will be empty—bare but not abandoned, as if an arrival or a return can always be anticipated. Sometimes, from inside the house, we face a window through which we see a strip of landscape or the meeting of sea and sky. But often the windows offer no view, confronting us with a bright but opaque screen and sometimes only with a rectangle of the deepest black.

*Joyce Zemans, *Christopher Pratt: A Retrospective* (Vancouver: Vancouver Art Gallery, 1985), p.24.

The Visitor brings us into the interior of the house. The tripartite division immediately casts ambiguity into the image: Is it the image of the room or the organizing strength of the rigid windowlike construction of the frame that has priority in the structure? The issue is made all the more tense because of the way that each element is viewed with absolute frontality. There are no angles of perspective as if we were scanning left and right across the surface; and the lighting on each object, too, is frontal and even. Ironically, this rigid frontality suggests that we could be looking in turn at each of the three walls of a room in which we stand against the fourth, unseen, wall.

Each of the objects that we see is a form of containment, but one in which the "contained" is either absent or obscure. We cannot see out of the window or into the drawers of the chest; the owner of the panties is elsewhere; and we do not know if there is heat coming from the duct. The only place where the link between the container and contained is explicit is the mysterious square marked on the wall in the central panel. These ambiguities and uncertainties within the elements extend into the title of the picture. Who is the visitor? Is it the owner of the panties whose presence we vicariously acknowledge? Or are we ourselves the visitor, imposing into a situation which, for all its banality, remains closed or obscured to us?

After saying in his description of his painting *House in August* "I get a sense of myself," Pratt continued: "The process is an act of research into one's own humanity. That's what the creative process is. You are researching a humanity, and the only humanity you have total access to is your own." The ambiguities in *The Visitor* are the divisions between what can be shown—that is, what we can describe as common within the experience of us all—and what is accessible only to each one of us as individuals, because of the isolation of our own experience.

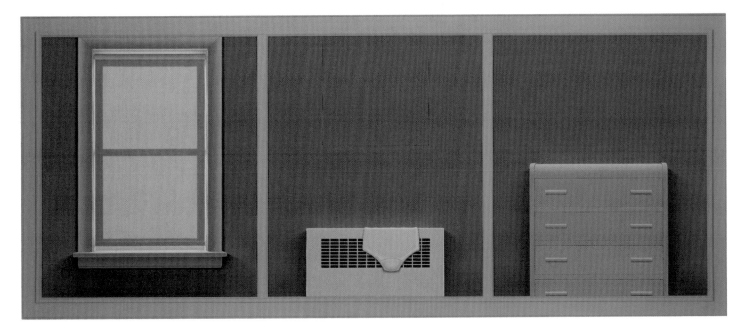

Christopher Pratt
The Visitor (1977),
oil on masonite, 94.6 × 226.8 cm assembled triptych
including frame.
Purchase, 1978.
Accession No. 23157.

Ivan Eyre

born 1935

Ivan Eyre is an outsider, an artist who has allegiance to no group, who resists categorization, who crosses boundaries. Ironically, to come to terms with the independence of Eyre's art, most people writing about his work have invoked a catalogue of other artists and the styles of earlier times. In a single passage, one writer was able to mention Francis Bacon, Giorgio De Chirico, Uccello, Piero della Francesca, Wyndham Lewis, Rogier van der Weyden, Picasso, African sculpture, Japanese prints, Egyptian carvings, George Grosz, Max Beckmann, Roberto Matta, Arshile Gorky, Cézanne, and Giotto. Eyre himself might acknowledge all of these (and might even suggest some that have been overlooked), but the references alone bring us no closer to his compelling and enigmatic work.

We can describe how, throughout his career, Eyre has painted still life, landscapes, and portraits. Sometimes these appear as separate genres, but often they are combined; and the more one sees of his work, the greater is the conviction that all his subjects belong to a single category. The relationship between the surface appearance of his work and the underlying forces that determine it is paralleled by the way he has written about the relationship between his art and his life: "As a painter I balance the chaos of sensations that informs my work with a structured, orderly life. . . . In my life I am pragmatic and cooperative, but the painting decisions are not *reasonable*—they do not form a theory that can be extracted from the work and used elsewhere."*

In the early 1970s, Eyre began to paint "pure" landscapes, closely worked pictures of substantial size. *Touchwood Hills*, made in 1973, is one of the earliest. Their detail and directness, in contrast to his ambiguous and "difficult" figure paintings, led some critics to assume a sharp break in his direction and a move towards realism. Yet in essential terms, the landscapes are an extension of his earlier work rather than a diversion from it. The further Eyre has developed them, the clearer it becomes that they must be seen in the context of his work alone, rather than in comparison to other contemporary landscape paintings.

*Joan Murray, *Ivan Eyre Exposition* (Oshawa: Robert McLaughlin Gallery, 1980), p.13.

Despite its apparent precision of view, *Touchwood Hills*, like all his landscapes, is an imaginary construction, based not on drawings or photographs, but composed in the studio from experience and memories. The format is curious, confining our scan of the landscape within an upright rectangle. Our viewpoint is high, and the sky is restricted to a very narrow band. This structure runs counter to the whole tradition of the prairie landscape painting, in which the emphasis has been on stressing the high skies and the piercing, clear light. Furthermore, this tradition, certainly in its modern manifestations, has favoured broad, freely painted surfaces. Eyre's painting, in contrast, is one of scrupulous detail, with the forms built up in tightly dotted strokes. The result is a hermetic surface with each element exactly and individually defined. The sky takes on a dun-green hue and casts its influence over the landscape. There are no shadows, only differences of density within the clumps of trees and undergrowth.

The result is an image of landscape that can only exist in our imagination, one of uncanny stillness, an absolute stillness. Yet this stillness must be reconciled with the viewpoint, one that first draws us above the landscape, drops us down sharply onto the plain and then, more slowly, sweeps us up towards the distant hills. The result is a powerful sense of tension between the kinetic drive of the viewpoint and immotile image of the land. Like the landscapes of dreams, it combines pleasure and fear, joining them in such a way that our reactions become uncertain, flickering from contentment to the darkest fears. In 1980, Eyre concluded an autobiographic essay: "In my recent work, particularly, the darkness has moved underground, but there are some who still see it lurking beneath the membrane of subject matter."**

**Ibid., p.35.

Ivan Eyre
Touchwood Hills (1972–73),
acrylic on canvas, 147.3 × 167.6 cm.
Purchase, 1974.
Accession No. 17658.

Michael Snow

born 1929

"My paintings are done by a filmmaker, sculpture by a musician, films by a painter, music by a filmmaker, paintings by a sculptor, sculpture by a filmmaker, films by a musician, music by a sculptor . . . sometimes they all work together."* For six years, between 1961 and 1967, Michael Snow dedicated his creative output to variations of a single image: a woman walking. The variants (several hundred of them, including some ephemeral "lost" works) appeared as paintings, sculptures, drawings, collages, installations, site works, and photographic works. Snow first developed the figure in October 1960—a silhouette cut from cardboard, with no details or features marked on it, and cropped at the wrists, ankles, and across the top of the head as though it had been enclosed by a picture frame. The image was at once an inversion of the process of Pop Art and a play on the Pygmalion myth. Pop Art transposed everyday objects into art, especially consumer objects. Snow's starting point, and the subject of the series, was already a work of art. The Pygmalion myth tells of a sculpture that came to life in response to the artist's desire; here, the reworking of art by art compounds the issue of art and reality.

*Michael Snow, in *Statements/18 Canadian Artists*, edited by Nancy E. Robertson (Regina: Norman Mackenzie Art Gallery, 1967), p.86.

In a technical sense, as one critic has said, Snow "asks Pirandello-like questions about the interplay between positive and negative, reverse and obverse, pictorial space and real space."** Snow has worked, creatively and professionally, as a painter, sculptor, filmmaker, and musician. The Walking Woman works were, as he has said, "an attempt to have variety." The desire for variety was manifested not only in the virtuosity of the presentations, abounding in visual and semantic puns, but also in the range of contexts in which the works were set. While these were often in the controlled situation of a gallery or museum, a number of works were set into a street or other public situation where the involuntary reactions of passers-by became part of the work.

**Kim Levin, quoted in *Walking Woman Works: Snow 1961–67* (Kingston: Agnes Etherington Art Centre, 1983), p.11.

Michael Snow
Clothed Woman (In Memory of my Father) (1963),
oil and lucite on canvas, 152.0 × 386.2 cm.
Purchase, 1966.
Accession No. 14946.

Snow made his first independent film in 1956 while working in the animation department of a Toronto film company. He lived in New York from 1962 to 1971, a period that roughly coincided with the Walking Woman works, and during this time he was heavily involved in experimental film. The crossover between his films and the Walking Woman works are complex and profound. *Clothed Woman (In Memory of my Father)*, painted in 1963, forms a filmlike sequence through its division into seven sections. Although we can discern part of the figure in each segment, the outline of the familiar shape is changed and even obscured by the use of colour. The sense of movement in the painting is thus a play between the dynamics of colour and line, which some- times unite and sometimes conflict.

In relation to the Walking Woman, Snow made a note to himself: "Revelation of process as subject. . . . Continue." Traditionally, art has revolved around the repetition of more or less fixed image structures—for instance, in religious art, portraiture, landscape, the female nude, and so on. In making his series around a fixed pictorial image, Snow critically examined the assumptions we make about subject, style, pictorial techniques, and iconography. In the Walking Woman works, the subject and the fundamental image remain fixed, but the process of the artist's presentation becomes the essential factor; that and the involvement of the viewer.

In *Authorization* of 1969, Snow pressed the issue further, specifically raising the question of the authority of the creator of the work and the position allowed for the viewer. He set up a Polaroid camera in front of a mirror and shot the image. He then glued the photo- graph to the top left of the area taped-off in the centre of the mirror and shot again. The second photograph thus includes himself and also the first shot glued to the mirror. He continued the process until the fifth image, which was glued to the upper left corner of the mirror.

An artist's work is about the artist working; it is his decision where to start and where to stop. But there is another factor (which we cannot see in this reproduc- tion of *Authorization*). In the actual work, we as observers are also reflected in the mirror. The process of the work implicates the viewer, literally reflecting us into what the artist has chosen to do. *Authorization* is a witty and critical exposure of the historical structure of art, which assumes that the authority of the artist is value- neutral—when in fact we cannot avoid taking his point of view.

Michael Snow
Authorization (1969),
black and white photographs and cloth tape on mirror in metal frame, 54.6 × 44.4 cm.
Purchase, 1969.
Accession No. 15839.

Joyce Wieland

born 1931

Until relatively recent years, there have been few women artists in Canada working at the leading edge of new art. Of these, fewer still have been recognized as asserting a perspective of their own rather than simply adding a "woman's touch" to the initiatives of their male colleagues. Thirty years ago, Joyce Wieland became one of these few. Not only was she making some of the most ambitious paintings of the time, but she was declaring through them a distinctive point of view, one that has marked all her work to the present, whether in film, assemblage, quilting, drawing, or painting. Through these media, she has asserted a personal voice on a wide range of feminist, political, nationalist, and ecological issues.

As with other young avant-garde artists in Toronto in the later 1950s, Wieland's early work was influenced by Abstract Expressionism. Out of this she produced a group of pictures, such as *Time Machine Series* of 1961 (Art Gallery of Ontario), which stand as very strong paintings and which also, by asserting powerful images of female sexuality, counter the macho attitudes that dominated Abstract Expressionism. Wieland moved to New York in 1962, broadening the range of her work in response to the artistic activity of that city. Her interest in filmmaking, begun in Toronto, became increasingly important, as did her work in collage and assemblage as she responded to Pop Art. Claes Oldenburg's "soft sculptures" had a strong influence on her.

Through living in New York for the better part of nine years while maintaining close ties with Toronto, Wieland became acutely conscious of her identity as a Canadian. She also became increasingly aware of her identity as a female artist in a male-oriented structure. She came to recognize her need to respond to both these experiences for their broad public implications as well as for their impact on her personally.

All these factors found a striking expression in the quiltworks that she made between 1966 and 1974. The quilts began in a modest way, formally extending the collaged clothworks she had made several years earlier. She began working with her sister, Joan Stewart, a quilt-maker, and she realized that more than simply extending her technical range, making the quilts engaged her in a co-operative working process and gave her access to a tradition of craftwork that had been reserved for women.

"Getting into the making of quilts as a woman's work was a conscious move on my part," she said. "It polarized my view of life; it made me go right into the whole feminine thing."* It was a bold step because it politicized Wieland's position as an artist. She was associating herself with an activity that had never had a place in the mainstream of art, and she faced this challenge by linking it to public statements of national identity.

Reason over Passion and its companion piece, *La Raison avant la passion*, drew on a speech by Pierre Trudeau, in which he had referred to the responsible behaviour of government. This and Wieland's other quiltworks balance wit with an assertive presentation of a traditional woman's craft in the context of fine art. *Reason over Passion* was included in Wieland's solo National Gallery exhibition of 1971, "True Patriot Love." The exhibition was significant in many ways, not least because it was the first the gallery had given to a living Canadian woman artist. It presented a strong statement with regard to the situation of being a woman artist and a Canadian, both in a general sense and in the particular ways in which Wieland gave expression to her individual identity through her work. In the years that have followed, the fundamental concerns have not changed, even as the particular statements she has made have evolved.

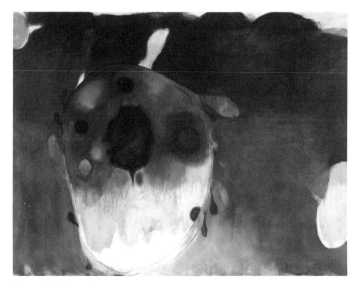

Joyce Wieland
Time Machine Series (1961),
oil on canvas, 203.2 × 269.9 cm.
Art Gallery of Ontario, Toronto.
Gift from the McLean Foundation, 1966.

*Joyce Wieland (Toronto: Art Gallery of Ontario/Key Porter, 1987), p.69.

Joyce Wieland
Reason over Passion (1968),
quilted cotton, 256.5 × 302.3 cm.
Purchase, 1970.
Accession No. 15924.

Betty Goodwin

born 1923

Etched vests, tarpaulin wall-hangings, room-sized and even house-sized installations, sculptures in steel, and figurative drawings, often on a very large scale. . . . A simple listing of the forms Betty Goodwin's work has taken seems to describe an artist with diffused and changeable concerns. But the experience of her work is one of being in contact with some of the most powerful, compelling, and integrated art that has been made in the last two decades. She has spoken about the cyclical process of her work: "Now, if you have gone through many cycles, they begin to resemble springs, in the sense that the first works in the cycle will force energy into the very last."*

*Betty Goodwin: Steel Notes, Canada 20th São Paulo International Biennial (Ottawa: National Gallery, 1989), p.113.

In 1982 she began the first in a series of figure drawings. She has made them on a range of supports (paper, vellum, translucent film) and in a mixture of media (pastel, oil, charcoal, graphite, crayon, gouache, wax). She builds up the figures, layer on layer, contrasting the materials, setting amorphous areas of colour against linear boundaries, often wiping forms away but never eliminating their traces. The figures we see are always in the process of becoming or in the process of dissolving. Her use of iridescent crayons, as the critic Robert Storr has said, "lend her flesh tones the peculiar sweetness and shimmer of putrefaction." Suffering, ecstatic, yearning, desolated, they are figures in physiological and psychological suspension. The earlier figures were swimmers, supported by their immersion in water but forced to seek air, threatened by their situation but recalling their origins floating in amniotic liquid. In the later drawings, the open gestures of the swimmers are lost and the figures are burdened, mutilated, able only to crawl on all fours. Images of erotic union are indistinguishable from violence; the desire for communication is negated by unbridgeable isolation; nakedness is not freedom but vulnerability.

Left: Betty Goodwin
Two Figures with Megaphone (1988),
mixed media on paper, 179.7 × 116.8 cm.
Collection of Christopher E. Horne.

Below: Betty Goodwin
Mentana Street Project, detail (1979).

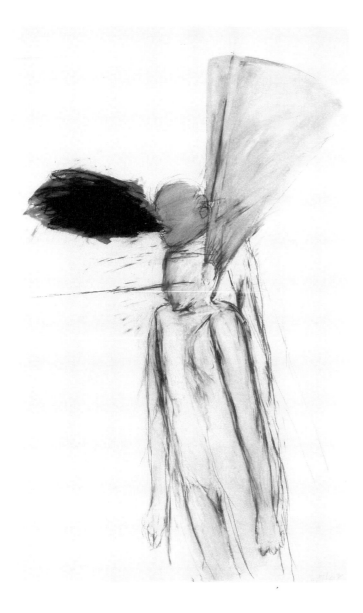

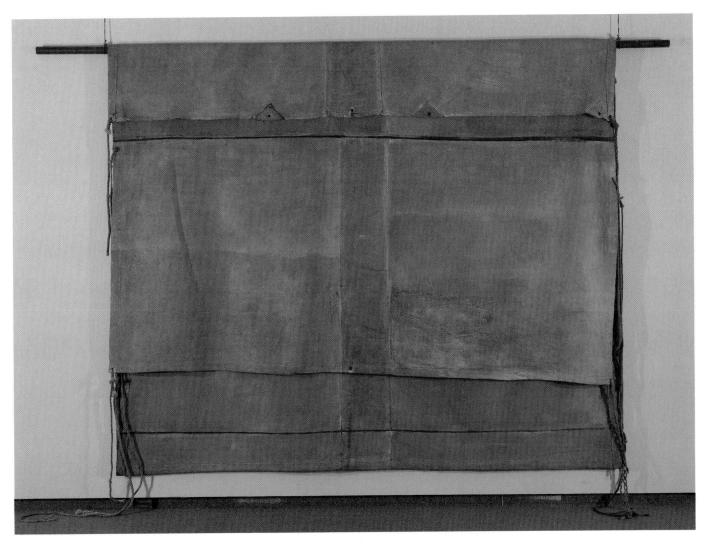

Betty Goodwin
Tarpaulin No. 3 (1975),
gesso, pastel, chalk, and charcoal on canvas with metal
grommets and rope, 231.0 × 293.5 cm.
Purchase, 1976.
Accession No. 18532.

Looking back through the cycle of these unsettling, sensitive figures, we see each stage of Goodwin's earlier works as the preparation towards them. But we have to be drawn to them, first, through objective references and analogy before we can face them directly as raw images of ourselves.

In the etchings that Goodwin made from 1969 to 1972, articles of clothing were pressed on the printing plate. The rich variations of light and dark that she gained in the prints created a pictorial illusion of space which conflicts ironically with our recognition of the garment as something made to enclose the volume of the human body. This sense of a material skin was extended in the group of tarpaulin wall-hangings made in 1975 and 1976, such as *Tarpaulin No. 3*. These were, in Marcel Duchamp's sense, "Rectified Ready Mades" in that Goodwin altered the existing objects—tarpaulins used to cover cargo—by patching and sewing them and working over their surfaces. Finally, they were folded and hung, suspended from the wall like skins no longer

young and fresh, but ones that were time-marked, worn, and mended. When she began the *Swimmers* she used animal skin, vellum, as the support for the drawings, hanging the sheets like the tarpaulins loosely from the wall.

If the etched garments and tarpaulins were objective reflections of the body—skinlike exteriors whose interiors were absent—the installations like *Rue Mentana* and *Passage in a Red Field* recast the emphasis so that the spectator, or rather the participant, gains an acute awareness of his or her own body. In the figure drawings of the 1980s, Goodwin sustains both the objective and subjective perspectives, bringing us to enter the fictional world of the drawings with an excruciating sense of our own physicality.

Paterson Ewen

born 1925

It is not a simple matter for an artist in his mid-forties to turn his back on twenty years of work and strike out in a new direction. It takes courage and a willingness to heed one's faculties of self-criticism. These are factors that characterize Paterson Ewen in relation to the work he has made since the early 1970s, work that has gained him considerable respect and attention both in Canada and abroad.

After wartime service in the army, Ewen went to McGill University to study geology. He was disillusioned by the approach taken to the subject and left after a year, switching his attention to art. During the first part of his career, he was deeply involved in the lively milieu of advanced art in Montreal. Through the 1950s, he was in the circle of young artists who associated themselves with Paul-Émile Borduas, and Ewen's work reflected an Automatiste approach. Later, he was among those artists at the leading edge of art in Montreal whose work shifted towards a reductive, geometric abstraction.

In 1968 Ewen left Montreal and settled in London, Ontario, which was the centre of a small but progressive art scene. Soon after this, he became dissatisfied with the direction of his work, recognizing that rather than fulfilling his own expression, he was simply following theoretical concerns that had been developed by other people. He began to experiment with new techniques in painting and saw how they were drawing him to images that had fascinated him since childhood, images of natural and cosmological phenomena. By 1971, he was making works that were as much mixed media as painting and whose subject matter was natural forces.

The significant change in Ewen's working methods came while he was carving a large sheet of plywood to make a woodcut print. He realized that the image he had cut and gouged in the wood could and should stand as the finished work. He began to work consistently by gouging the image into plywood (first by hand and subsequently with an electric router), then applying paint, and often adding other materials such as metal and cloth. The subjects he chose—rain storms, wind storms, lightning strikes—were thus formed from combining the rough, graphic structure of the gouged plywood with subtle and evocative painting. As he continued to work, he extended the range of his subject matter to deal with cosmological events, such as comets, shooting stars, and sunbursts, as well as the starry sky, nebulae, and the moon.

Ewen's paintings have great physical presence. They are large-scale, often two or three metres wide, and on heavy-gauge plywood. Their toughness shows in the coarse texture of the plywood and in the ripped, splintered tracks of the router. The raw character of the surfaces, combined with the sensitivity of the painting, superbly reflects the awesome beauty we experience from the forces of nature.

Gibbous Moon is one of a group of pictures that Ewen made with the moon as the subject. The title refers to a phase in the moon's cycle when the illuminated part is between a semicircle and a full circle ("gibbous" derives from the Latin for "hunched"). Ewen has etched the shape of the moon by carving away the whole area surrounding it and painting that area dark blue. By contrasting the blue with its complementary colour, orange, he heightens the illusion of three-dimensionality; and by the carefully formed asymmetry of the moon's shape, he impresses on us its dynamics, suggesting both its axial rotation and its movement through space.

Ewen's disappointment when he began studying geology was with the prosaic way the subject was treated, its reduction to formulae. Subsequently, in his art of the fifties and sixties, his own interests were enclosed within the broader context of the advanced art of the day. But his fascination with natural and cosmic phenomena remained, and he came to realize that he had to deal with this directly in his art. The solution he has come to is one that steps between the scientific and mythological: he deals with a reality that retains its mystery.

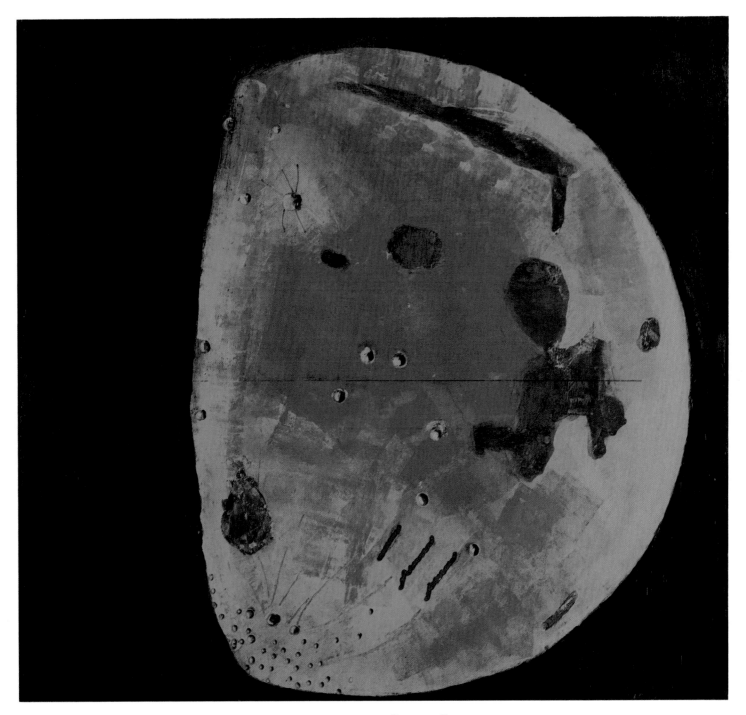

Paterson Ewen
Gibbous Moon (1980),
acrylic on gouged plywood, 228.6 × 243.8 cm.
Purchase, 1980.
Accession No. 23659.

Guido Molinari

born 1933

The exhibition "Espace 55" became the occasion for a strenuous dispute between Paul-Émile Borduas and Fernand Leduc. Borduas, then living in New York, criticized the current state of painting in Montreal; Leduc took exception to this, pointing out the leading role that Borduas had played in Montreal art since the early 1940s. Guido Molinari, then only twenty-one, entered the debate with an article which, taking Borduas's argument as a starting point, proposed a much more radical perspective. Finding that Montreal Automatism was still linked to a structure of traditional three-dimensional space, Molinari argued that a new approach to space had already been initiated by Mondrian and Pollock. He called for a further advance on the positions they had established by the creation of a pictorial space that arose from what he described as "colour-light."

The same year, Molinari sought to break the vestiges of traditional illusionistic space with some radical black and white paintings. The following year, 1956, he made a group of hard-edge paintings, the most striking of which is *Angle noir*. This large painting was uncompromising in its reductive, geometric form and in its absolute contrast between black and white, between light and the absence of light. The strength of the black-white contrast and the balance of shape introduced a tension that could only be resolved in its own terms, not by reference to an illusion of the natural world such as remained even in the abstract paintings of the Automatistes. Molinari asserted that there should be no gradual loosening of the bonds to the past; a new approach to space must begin with a decisive proposition. Only in that way was it possible for painting to make an independent statement rather than continuing to depend on the traditional perspectives by which art represented meaning about the world. *Angle noir* was a bold and confident move. The position it opened is one that Molinari has pursued rigorously in the decades since. As he wrote later, "Space is a form in itself, and space is consequently an unlimited mutation."

Guido Molinari
Angle noir (1956),
enamel paint on canvas, 152.4 × 183.0 cm.
Purchase, 1967.
Accession No. 15236.

The problem of "colour-light" was first fully examined in several series of paintings that Molinari made through the 1960s. In formal terms, these consisted principally of contiguous vertical stripes of colour. But the formal structure was a means and not an end; it was simply a way of delivering the colour. Because all the stripes in a particular picture were always equal in size and shape, the activity within the pictures rested wholly on the spectator's perception of colour.

The *Rhythmic Mutation No. 9* of 1965 uses five colours—green, red, blue, orange, and a deep cadmium red. These are repeated in shifting and unequal relationships, so that while the green and blue are repeated five times and the orange four times, the cadmium red and the red appear only three times. As we scan back and forth across the surface, our eye responds to a complex rhythm that is created not only by the asymmetrical repetition of colours but also by the shifting qualities of the colours as they stand in different relationships to one another. It is a rhythm in mutation, forming a dynamic space which relies only on the perception of colour.

Shortly before this painting was made, Molinari spoke about the relationships between literature and painting. He said that, in poetry, "the word takes on its total shape and multiple meanings, and thereby loses its object-identity. Colour is to painting what the word is to poetry. That is the reason why I do not work on the form . . . but the colour which determines the form. By losing its identity, the word attains the full value, as was shown so well by Mallarmé."*

*Pierre Théberge, *Guido Molinari* (Ottawa: National Gallery, 1976), p.41.

Guido Molinari
Rhythmic Mutation No. 9 (1965),
acrylic on canvas, 203.2 × 152.4 cm.
Purchase, 1975.
Accession No. 18484.

Claude Tousignant

born 1932

In 1956, Claude Tousignant, then twenty-four years old, held an exhibition of his new paintings at the Galerie L'Actuelle in Montreal. They were a startling group of works—geometric forms set down as large, powerful areas of colour, which both shaped and were shaped by the format of the pictures. Their uncompromising abstraction made them among the most radical works of their time: *Monochrome orange* was a field of absolutely evenly applied intense orange, while *Le Lieu d'infini* comprised a rectangular black plane, edged top and bottom with wide red bands.

Tousignant had studied at the school of design of the Musée des Beaux-Arts in Montreal from 1948 to 1951 and had then gone to Paris. For an older generation of Montreal abstract artists—Borduas, Riopelle, Fernand Leduc—Paris remained, to a greater or lesser degree, the essential artistic and intellectual source. But Tousignant was disappointed by what he saw, and his stay there led him to recognize the North American character of his roots. Back in Montreal in 1953, his first paintings were freely developed, gestural abstracts which acknowledged an Automatiste heritage but without its Surrealist overtones. The Plasticien group, led by Rodolphe de Repentigny, began to make hard-edged paintings in 1954. The following year, Tousignant and Guido Molinari took a far more rigorous approach to abstraction, standing against the Cubist space and the Plasticiens' tendency towards decorativeness.

Tousignant firmly declared his direction in a statement he wrote for an exhibition catalogue in 1959: "What I wish to do is to make painting objective, to bring it back to its source—where only painting remains, emptied of all extraneous matter—to the point at which painting is pure sensation."* The severely reductive character of his art was to remove everything ambiguous or referential so that the spectator would begin by viewing an object that was distinct and autonomous.

*Danielle Corbeil, *Claude Tousignant* (Ottawa: National Gallery, 1973), p.14.

In the early 1960s, Tousignant experimented with a variety of approaches before returning to hard-edged forms and strong colours. Later, he was to move away from the traditional square or rectangular format, and to make paintings in the form of circles and other shapes. The impetus that gave him direction came from the work of Barnett Newman, whose paintings created space by the mass and quality of their colour. This led Tousignant to look back to his 1956 paintings, finding in them the potential for new directions. After working through various forms, in which he used circular motifs within rectangular canvases, he made his first circular format paintings in 1965, and over the next few years he painted several groups of such works, investigating the range of possibilities raised by the relationships among the coloured rings.

Accélérator chromatique of 1967 is from the third group of these circular paintings. The series of colours he establishes are moved through various sequences of relationships. The juxtaposition of the colours and their position on the canvas radically change our perception of any individual colour, while the pulsing, dynamic structure causes our eyes to mix the colours, multiplying their range and recasting their character. At this point, the painting defies description, for its existence has been recreated by the experience of the viewer to become pure sensation.

Claude Tousignant
Accélérator chromatique (1967),
acrylic on canvas, 244.7 cm diameter.
Purchase, 1967.
Accession No. 15319.

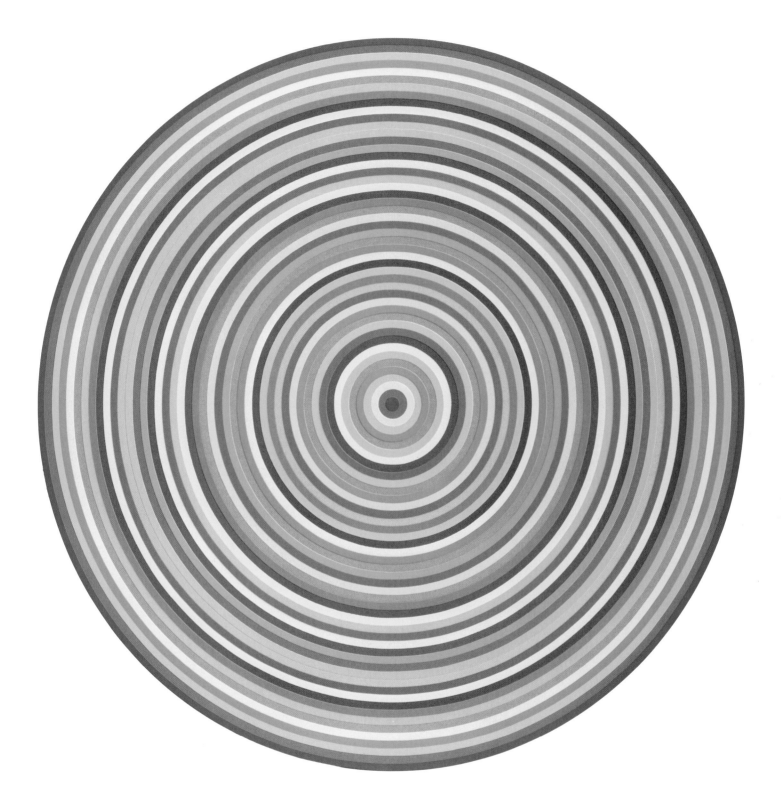

Dennis Burton

born 1933

Regional isolation and an enduring conservatism saw modernist innovation in Canadian art erupt as abrupt shifts in direction brought about by small groups of artists rather than emerging from a context of diversity. What this actually meant for a young artist beginning to develop his career was described with clarity and honesty by Dennis Burton in the essay he wrote for the catalogue of his retrospective exhibition at the Robert McLaughlin Gallery, Oshawa.

The situation faced by Burton and his peers, the "second generation" of modernists in Toronto, was curious in that the breakthroughs made by the "first generation," the Painters Eleven, occurred when the "second generation" were students. (Burton graduated from the Ontario College of Art in 1956.) It was thus not a question of the younger artists reacting against their older colleagues, for they were all looking towards the same horizon of advanced art at much the same time—reading *Art News* and other magazines, going to New York and to the Albright-Knox Art Gallery in Buffalo, and picking up on the Abstract Expressionists.

The full story of this period of art in Toronto has yet to be told, in particular the relationship between the development of abstraction and the fact that for both generations of artists the human figure and landscape remained central to their concerns. Burton was making some striking abstracts in the late 1950s—gestural, attacking pictures—while by the mid-1960s he had moved to explicitly figurative images. He has described the directness of the relationship between immediate experience and painting, for instance, in the importance that the urban scene has for him, specifically the downtown scene: the textures and patterns and colours seen in the dilapidated areas of the city, "from broken windows stuffed with rags to windows with cardboard stained by the rain, to the look of scratched bricks, to painted graffiti." He linked these visual situations to the painters who interested him, for "I'm painting the same kind of subject matter the New York abstract expressionists painted."[*]

Burton gained wide attention with the "Garterbelt-mania" exhibition at the Isaacs Gallery in 1965. The images were based on photographs from New York "skin books," which Burton abstracted to flat shapes with strong, textureless areas of colour. He wrote: "I had just depicted the female in underwear which at the time I suppose was a way to shock the middle class. But underwear was not just for its own sake; it was a matter of getting an obsession and a 'hang-up' out of my system."[**] In fact, he had begun making erotic drawings some years earlier and had included in his first one-man show a major painting, *The Game of Life*, made in the fall of 1960. He has described how the motivation for the picture came from an exhibition of African sculpture at the Isaacs Gallery.

The painting is organized like a board game, with the "pieces" set out as they might be at the start: lips, breasts, penises, and vulvae collected in their quadrants, with the artist's handprints in the "lips" section. Burton said that the painting was "a fight against facility by making a very loose, almost childlike work." Its structure is reminiscent of the "pictographs" of the American artist Adolph Gottlieb, which Gottlieb said "puts us at the beginning of seeing." But unlike the detachment of Gottlieb's pictures, Burton's *The Game of Life* is activated by the tensions and energy of sexual dynamics.

[**]*Ibid.*, p.23.

[*]*Dennis Burton: Retrospective* (Oshawa: Robert McLaughlin Gallery, 1977), p.39.

Dennis Burton
The Game of Life (1960),
oil on canvas, 137.4 × 198.3 cm.
Purchase, 1968.
Accession No. 15444.

Graham Coughtry

born 1931

The general assumption in distinguishing the advanced from the conservative painting of the 1950s and 1960s is that it was a conflict between abstract art and representational imagery. But if this was true in Montreal, it was not so in Toronto, where figurative subject matter was gaining renewed vigour. For none of the younger painters was this more true than for Graham Coughtry, whose richly painted canvases have taken the human figure as their constant theme.

Coughtry graduated from the Ontario College of Art in 1953. Over the next six years, absorbing a wide range of visual ideas, he gradually moved towards the development of an individual image. He was drawn to the work of Velázquez, Bonnard, and Monet; and through Bonnard (the epitome of the painter's painter), he realized how painting could be an end in itself. Visits to New York brought him into contact with American Abstract Expressionism, and, not surprisingly, it was the work of Willem de Kooning that most impressed him. He said, "The thing about de Kooning that has always been important to me is the way he turned the image into an actual way of painting, spread it all over the canvas, and still retained traces of what the image was to begin with."*

Through the 1950s, while working for a graphics company and the CBC, Coughtry became involved in film, and this became a major impetus in the development of his imagery. Specifically, what interested him (referring back to the photo-sequences of Eadweard Muybridge) was how human motion was captured by the individual frames of a film. From his study of the painters he admired, and from his interest in the figure in motion, came the painting *Emerging Figure* of 1959. This image is a sort of Venus Anadyomene, but instead of rising out of the sea, Coughtry's figure gathers its form out of the abstract painterly surface that surrounds it.

The combination of rich sensuous painting and erotic imagery in a large-scale format characterizes the *Two Figures* series, which gained Coughtry considerable attention and positive critical notice. Begun in 1962, the series was shown at the Isaacs Gallery in 1964. Coughtry said that it was "very definitely an attempt to depict a sexual confrontation between two figures . . . an attempt to transform sexual imagery into a way of painting."** Or, to extend the analogy, it was a way of transforming sexual energy into a way of painting.

*Barrie Hale, *Graham Coughtry Retrospective* (Oshawa: Robert McLaughlin Gallery, 1976), p.9.
**Ibid., p.14.

The compositional structure is similar throughout the series. In *Two Figures No. 5*, the figures cut diagonally across the canvas, dividing the field into upper and lower sections, which are differentiated in colour and thinly painted, with streaks flowing down the surface. The limbs of the figures stretch beyond the boundaries of the picture, as if seeking a secure anchor in the rectangular shape of the canvas. From its relative thinness in the outer parts, the paint gathers, layer on layer, towards the centre, where the two intertwined figures become individually indistinguishable. The paint does not illustrate the image; rather, paint and image are direct equivalents of artistic and bodily activities.

The ambiguous frenzy of passion—between the ecstasy of pleasure and the violence of pain—gives way to a slower rhythm in the later works of the series. The focus of ambiguity shifts to the blending of the two figures until, in *Two Figures No. 21*, they become a single form sharing a common outline. This more lyrical approach led into Coughtry's next group of paintings, but the extraordinary daring and intensity of the *Two Figures* series was lost.

For four years from 1967, while living on Ibiza, one of the Balearic Islands, Coughtry did no painting, although he continued to draw. When he returned to Toronto and began painting again, it was partly a matter of reclaiming the place where he had broken off and partly a matter of reconstructing the process of painting and its image. As he progressed with his series called *Water Figures*, which was based on shots from movies he had made of a young girl playing in the sea, the figure was dissolved until it was no longer discernible. Then, in the mid-1970s, following some "over-all" abstract paintings, the figure re-emerged in the painting *Reclining Figure Moving, No. 25*.

Graham Coughtry
Two Figures No. 5 (1962),
oil and lucite on canvas, 177.6 × 127.0 cm.
Purchase, 1963.
Accession No. 9991.

Gordon Rayner

born 1935

Gordon Rayner followed the tradition that was established by members of the Group of Seven and continued by the Painters Eleven, by which advanced painters in Toronto began their career as commercial artists. Rayner served part of his apprenticeship with Jack Bush, through whom he came to follow the moves towards abstraction that the Painters Eleven were making, particularly their response to New York Abstract Expressionism. The Painters Eleven, in their six-year existence, brought art in Toronto forward by several decades. Younger artists such as Rayner, Dennis Burton, Graham Coughtry, and others could meet the challenge of their work and take as their point of departure the radical art of New York: Abstract Expressionism and, beyond that, Neo-Dadaism, "happenings," and performances.

Rayner's has always been an exuberant, witty, and generous art. It has ranged widely in style and image, a characteristic that has brought him praise for inventiveness and suspicion for inconsistency. It is a range in honest response to his experience—to life in downtown Toronto, to his love of the northern wilderness, to the sights and colours drawn from his travels in many parts of the world. In formal and technical terms, this has often led him to deny strict adherence to traditional formats and traditional materials. He has painted on shaped canvases, has made assemblages and collages, and has used materials ranging from an old pair of jeans to typographers' cases, and to rulers, rocks, and neon. He was making "assemblages" before he had seen the work of Robert Rauschenberg, and he was integrating drawings and paintings by his contemporaries into his own works long before the term "appropriation" had gained its current loaded sententiousness.

Rayner himself, thinking about the criticism of his work being too varied, said that its consistency lay in "a certain kind of colour, a certain touch and a certain image." In a more specific way, one can say that so much of Rayner's work, whether in an abstract or representational form, has been concerned with a personal, painterly expression of the northern landscape. For several years as a child he went to a summer cottage, "Charlie's" cabin, in the Magnetawan district near Parry Sound. In the mid-1950s he established a pattern of going to this place year after year and making paintings and drawings there.

In many essential respects, the character of all Rayner's visual experience—whether drawn from Toronto, from across Canada, or from Mexico, Spain, or the Far East—has been told through his deep attachment to this area of northern Ontario. Sometimes the experience of the Magnetawan landscape has been expressed directly and immediately. Such was the case with *Magnetawan No. 2*. This painting is one of three that he kept from a group he made in response to a particular experience—a massive thunderstorm. "It was one of the occasions where an actual experience was so profound and so much a part of my life that I decided to do some paintings about it. It's seldom that I do that."* The result is one of the most dramatic paintings of such an occurrence, with the violence of the storm brilliantly imagined in the clear white flashes on the black, and the way the power of the event transforms all the other colours of the landscape. Through the well-chosen use of the diamond format, Rayner has combined the awesome piling of the cumulo-nimbus clouds and the flashing lightning, with the panorama of the landscape.

*Joan Murray, *Gordon Rayner Retrospective* (Oshawa: Robert McLaughlin Gallery, 1978), p.38.

Gordon Rayner
Magnetawan No. 2 (1965),
acrylic on canvas, 162.0 × 162.0 × 4.0 cm diamond;
159.8 × 159.8 cm measured square.
Purchase, 1967.
Accession No. 15315.

Greg Curnoe

born 1936

In the 1960s, London, Ontario, became the centre of a small but radical and ambitious art scene. This was the result of the energy and talent of a few young artists, sustained not by their adherence to a group style or program but by the collective strength of their diversity and individuality. Greg Curnoe was at the core of this activity. In 1961, soon after establishing his own studio, he founded the magazine *Region*, and the following year he set up, with other London artists, an artist-run gallery. His studio became "a vital meeting place for a whole generation of artists."*

In naming his magazine *Region*, Curnoe made an early statement on a political and artistic concern that has been central to his life and his work. Talking about art as "regionalist" so often becomes a way of describing (and dismissing) activity that is, at best, thought of as being on the margins of the mainstream, following at a distance with a loss of intensity the innovations generated in the main centres. Curnoe revised the meaning of "regionalism," moving it away from the stigma of the unsophisticated and towards the reality that the individual artist must always work from his or her resources within a particular context and environment. Regionalism in Curnoe's terms has meant seizing that reality. He wrote: "I believe that the artists who are original, who break out of the colonial mould, are the ones who really affect our culture and inevitably they are original because they develop out of their whole background."** This does not mean a narrow-minded dismissal of values from elsewhere, but it does mean rejecting the uncritical assumption that what comes from outside forms the standard by which one should operate. In particular, as Curnoe has made clear in his work, his writings, and his lectures, this has meant refusing American values as the arbiter of Canadian culture.

This criticism of outside values as the standard has included the rejection of "high art," the notion of an inevitable and elitist level of art. Working from one's "whole background" means working from an awareness of one's own circumstances and the reality of one's position within popular culture. It means asserting a position based on the directness of everyday experience. Curnoe reflects this in his work through the range of his interests as expressed in a diversity of approaches in different techniques of painting, drawing, collage, assemblage, and mixed media.

The openness of Curnoe's approach is well shown by two related works in the National Gallery: *View of Victoria Hospital, First Series: No. 1–6* of 1969 and *View of Victoria Hospital, Second Series*, 1969–71. The First Series consists of six very large canvases covered with stamped lettering forming a sort of stream of consciousness that describes the view of Victoria Hospital in London, as seen from Curnoe's studio. The Second Series is a mixed-media work. The basis is a view of the hospital and its environs painted in a colourful, simplified illustrative style. Various locations are marked on the painting by numbers which refer to particular events of significance in Curnoe's experience; a notebook displayed with the painting lists out the topics to which the numbers refer. A tape of sounds recorded in his studio plays through loudspeakers set into the upper part of the painting. The work is autobiographical, yet we are aware that while it presents a particular point of view—Curnoe's point of view—it does so around a building that is very familiar to the population of the city. The events and thoughts are Curnoe's, but his engagement with this space and place parallels that of so many other people. The upbeat, billboard style of the painting supports this sense of accessibility, and the relationship he draws between personal and collective experience reflects how Curnoe lives and works his definition of regionalism.

*Pierre Théberge, *Greg Curnoe* (Ottawa: National Gallery, 1982), p.7.
**Ibid., p.17.

Greg Curnoe
View of Victoria Hospital, Second Series (February 10, 1969–March 10, 1971) (1969–71),
oil, rubber stamp and ink, graphite, and wallpaper on plywood, under plexiglas, with audiotape, tape player, and eight-page text (photocopied from a rubber-stamped notebook), 243.8 × 487.0 cm assembled.
Purchase, 1970.
Accession No. 16894.

Greg Curnoe
View of Victoria Hospital, First Series: No. 1–6 (1968–69),
rubber stamp and ink over latex on canvas; each 289.6 × 228.6 cm.
National Gallery of Canada.

Charles Gagnon

born 1934

In France, the Court of Cassation is the supreme court of appeal with the power to quash the decisions of other courts. In English, "cassation" means the action of making null and void. Why would Charles Gagnon use *Cassation* as the title for a group of paintings he made in the 1970s?

Gagnon was born and brought up in Montreal. He became interested in photography as a boy and has pursued this interest professionally as a photographer and teacher. He once wrote: "I believe that photography has had a greater effect on my painting than vice versa, and this on a philosophical basis rather than a 'formal' one."* The crucial time in his early artistic development came in the five years from 1955 that he spent in New York—studying, taking photographs, painting, looking. It was a lively time in advanced art in New York, the time of "happenings" and "environments," of John Cage and Merce Cunningham, the time when the dominance of Abstract Expressionist painting was coming under challenge from the early work of Jasper Johns and Robert Rauschenberg.

Gagnon's New York photographs concentrated on the decaying city—on cracked plaster, peeling walls, graffiti, debris. His paintings of the same period, with their rough-textured surfaces and curious markings, in part reflected the themes of his photographs and in part recalled the calligraphy of ancient languages. Both the photographs and the paintings draw our attention to the edges and margins of things, rather than to their

*Philip Fry, *Charles Gagnon* (Montreal: Montreal Museum of Fine Arts, 1978), p.25.

obvious centre. They unsettle our assumptions of the security of a seamless world by presenting us with images of disjunctures and gaps. In paintings of the 1960s, Gagnon used windowlike structures to allude to breaches between inner and outer spaces, creating a tension between the actual surfaces of the paintings and the illusions they suggest.

During the 1970s, Gagnon developed two groups of paintings, the *Cassations* and the *Splitscreens*. The first took the form of a rectangle within a rectangle, as if one were looking through a doorway or from a window, while the *Splitscreens* comprise a series of horizontal bands, somewhat like the frames of a film that have slipped out of alignment. Both groups are built up in richly layered, gesturally applied paint; the paint defines the formal divisions within the paintings and yet retains the primacy of the "all-over" surface. However much we are drawn to read spatial illusion in the works, we can never escape their literal, abstract qualities.

Cassation, whether in the legal sense or in the broader meaning of rendering null and void, implies taking a position that stands above or outside a particular state of affairs; it implies being able to make a judgement that, in negating what has gone before, asserts a new level. The *Cassation* paintings open into illusion, into the potential of one space opening to another, and at the same time they quash that illusion through the literal fact of the painting itself, which asserts the artistic process of applying material to a flat surface. In the title of the National Gallery picture *Cassation/Open/Ouvert*, Gagnon plays on the words at two levels: first, that the word "cassation" is the same in English and French, though with different usages, while "open/ouvert" has the same meaning but is rendered by different words; second, that it is hard to reconcile the finality of cassation with the promise of openness. Yet it is this apparent contradiction that describes the painting, which is literally finite and resolved, yet always open, always promising.

Charles Gagnon
Cassation/Open/Ouvert (1976),
oil on canvas, 203.2 × 330.2 cm.
Purchase, 1976.
Accession No. 18666.

Yves Gaucher

born 1934

Distinctions among the works of reductive abstract painters are marked less by the particular formal structures they use than by the pictorial spaces they create. Colour and shape are functions of space, determining the particular quality and character of the work and opening it to the psychological and physiological responses that belong only to the experience of the individual viewer.

Although Gaucher was born in Montreal and grew up there during a time of considerable radical movement in the visual arts, he was not involved with the debates and activities surrounding such groups as the Automatistes and the Plasticiens. Maintaining a distance was a matter of both choice and temperament. He knew he had to develop in his own terms, separately from group activity and from the arguments about theoretical positions. His way of proceeding, by concentrating on printmaking rather than painting in the early years of his career, was characteristic. This decision was not so much because it was "the type of work he would produce for the future, but a style of working which would also characterize his painting procedure." As Gaucher said, the print medium "allowed time to reflect and rectify decisions."*

In Paris in 1962 he went to a concert that included music by Anton von Webern. This experience, he said, "challenged every single idea I had about sound, about art, about expression, about the dimensions all these things could have. . . . The music seemed to send little cells of sound into space, where they expanded and took on a whole new quality and dimension of their own."**

The result of this experience was a remarkable set of relief prints, *En Hommage à Webern*. Comprising linear and square forms, some inked and some not, some embossed and some pressed into the paper, the prints dispose geometric structures that are not resolvable in a surface pattern; they can only be resolved through a dynamic of spatial perception.

Since the mid-1960s, Gaucher has made various series of paintings in which he pursues particular formal and coloristic problems. The most remarkable of these early series are the grey-on-grey paintings, such as *T-PB-11 J-JN-69*. Begun in December 1967 and ended in October 1969, the series consists of forty paintings. They all have grey grounds, smoothly and evenly laid down, interspersed with short horizontal lines (what Gaucher came to call "signals") which are also painted in shades of grey. While the signals are made from mixtures of black and white, the grey fields are tinted, and although these colour effects are barely perceptible, they give the paintings a sense of warmth or coolness. The paintings are large (*T-PB-11 J-JN-69* is about two metres high and over three and a half metres wide) so that to the viewer they become, as Gaucher has said, "not paintings anymore but environment conditions." Standing in front of such a painting, with one's eye settled to the neutral ground, one becomes aware of the grey signals. Like the forms in the Webern prints, the horizontal lines seem to exist at different depths within the grey field. Some advance firmly, some recede, and some seem to appear and disappear as one's eye scans around the surface. Gradually—for the experience of the painting is gained slowly—the apparently chance appearance of the signals establishes a rhythm, one that is formed by the viewer's subjective responses to the interaction of the greys on grey.

The Webern prints alluded directly to music, as did a series of paintings Gaucher made in 1967, the *Ragas*. This title refers to the traditional Hindu melodic form and is from the Sanskrit word meaning colour or mood. Gaucher's original title for the grey paintings was *Alap*, the opening of a *Raga*, until he changed to shorthand designations of the colours used and the dates of each painting. Still, it seems natural to use terms such as tone, value, and rhythm in reference to the pictures. The musical references, however, are an analogy rather than a description (just as the "window" in traditional painting makes an analogy to the natural world). The essence of the paintings lies in the viewer's physical and psychological experience of an autonomous space. The viewer who takes the time to absorb a painting such as *T-PB-11 J-JN-69* gains an experience that is among the most moving offered by recent painting.

*Roald Nasgaard, *Yves Gaucher: A Fifteen-year Perspective 1963–1978* (Toronto: Art Gallery of Ontario, 1979), p.29.
**Ibid., p.20.

Yves Gaucher
T-PB-11 J-JN-69 (1969),
acrylic on canvas, 202.7 × 366.3 cm.
Purchase, 1987.
Accession No. 29841.

Murray Favro

born 1940

A substantial number of artists throughout this century have been concerned with stretching, disrupting, reforming, and redefining the character and values of the visual arts. For some, the changes in their way of looking and working have been brought about as a result of chance experiences; others have launched deliberate campaigns that call the conventions of art into question—and have then questioned the critical positions they have taken. Still others have re-evaluated the boundaries of art through the very processes by which they work, taking advantage of the way they can critically examine technical or social issues with a freedom that is precluded by the demands of the everyday world. It is in this last sense that the radical contributions of Murray Favro have been made.

Favro is an inventor, in the sense of being a *bricoler*, a tinkerer (a title by which Marcel Duchamp also described himself). His projects include many that reflect his interest in aeronautics: a *Propeller Testing Machine*, 1966; a *Propeller Engine*, 1978; a half-sized *Sabre Jet*. He has made electric guitars and works that involve projecting coloured slides onto three-dimensional constructions, most notably the witty and intriguing *Van Gogh's Room*, 1973–74 (Art Gallery of Ontario). In these and other works, his constructions and reconstructions investigate unrealized (and often unrealizable) aspects of technology, or they open new angles on the perception of the natural world and the world of art, or comment on the social meaning of mass-production.

If the process of Favro's work is that of a *bricoler*, the values of his projects can be described as *bricoles*, not in the sense of trifles but as a term deriving from Real Tennis, meaning an unexpected stroke or action. This is the core of his work; for what at first may appear to be a curious or tangential comment on an aspect of technology, or on the everyday world, becomes in a Favro project a surprising and revealing analysis of a situation that we conventionally overlook or take for granted.

Synthetic Lake of 1972–73 was inspired by the common and fascinating pastime of watching waves break on a shore. While most of us are content to be lulled by the mesmerizing rhythm, Favro's thoughts moved in another direction: "The motion . . . was something I wanted to cause mechanically."* His immediate idea was to combine a movie film loop with a structure that would reproduce a wave motion. By means of an extended series of drawings, he formally analysed the motion and then sought to transform these abstractions into a mechanical structure.

His solution was to set groups of hinged wooden slats in a series linked to an auger-shaped shaft that was turned by an electric motor. A length of canvas was draped over the wooden device so that, as the shaft revolved, the canvas moved up and down in a wavelike sequence. He then projected a film loop of breaking waves onto the canvas. The concept of the work was not an attempt at *trompe-l'oeil*, a means of persuading us that the room containing the structure was in fact filled with breaking waves; rather, it was a way of playing on the differences between the natural and the mechanical production of waves in order to create a tension between perception and understanding. Our curiosity about the workings of this strange machine reflects Favro's curiosity about the mystery of the forces that produce the natural phenomenon of breaking waves. The combination of the crude device and the illusion of the projected film contrast with the unified assumptions we make about our perception and our understanding of a natural state of affairs. *Synthetic Lake* is a bricole, an unexpected rebound that opens a gap of uncertainty between what we see and what we are conditioned to assume.

*Marie Fleming, *Murray Favro: A Retrospective* (Toronto: Art Gallery of Ontario, 1983), p.60.

Murray Favro
Van Gogh's Room (1973–74),
wood, slides (multimedia piece), 259.2 × 365.7 × 365.6 cm.
Art Gallery of Ontario, Toronto.

Murray Favro
Synthetic Lake (1972–73),
16 mm colour film loop, projector, wave-machine constructed
of wood, canvas, rope, electric motor, and metal fittings,
2.9 × 6.1 × 12.2 m installation space, including projection;
wave-machine, 89.5 × 300.9 × 446.4 cm.
Purchase, 1974.
Accession No. 17969.

Gathie Falk

born 1928

Boots and shoes, herds of galloping horses, thermal blankets, richly flowering gardens, snapshots from family albums, saddles bearing a basket of eggs or a pile of cups and saucers. . . . These are among the subjects of Gathie Falk, subjects which reflect simple commonplace objects that are translated from their everyday contexts and transposed into painting, ceramic, and drawing.

Falk has spoken about her art as being a "personal vision of things already in the world."* It is personal, certainly, but it is linked to the experience of us all, because the objects we see and use, no matter how banal they seem, are attached by invisible threads to the lives we lead. Isolate those objects from the way we encounter them in our everyday lives, revise their appearance by representing them in changed materials, and they form a new context that challenges our conventions. In particular, their presentation as works of art in a gallery or museum setting gives them the character of precious objects or objects of celebration—as Falk has said, it is the "veneration of the ordinary."

The process Falk uses in her choice of subject and in the presentation of her work has Surrealist overtones: the surprise and often the humour in objects wrenched from their context; the way we can be forced to recognize the relativity in our lives by disturbing the boundaries of the everyday to make way for magic. Her *Herd Two* of 1975 (National Gallery)—a herd of twenty-four white-painted plywood horses, their features drawn on

with pencil—arose from a combination of two events: she had been intrigued by a carousel-type horse she had seen at the entrance to a Safeway store; and she linked this image with the twenty-four clouds she had used as props in one of her performance works. Joining these two together, she has drawn us into the childhood experience that transforms a mechanical ride into a world of make-believe.

The idea for the *Eight Red Boots* came from a glass-fronted display case filled with shoes, which Falk saw outside a shoe store. She changed the simple case into a wall-mounted cabinet, the type one might see in someone's home as a place to hold a treasured collection of ornaments. The boots, in deep-red glazed ceramic, are like ornaments—but of a disturbing scale. Rather than being charming miniatures, they are full-sized models of used boots (or boots that are still in use), with creased leather and with zips undone as if their owners had just stepped out of them. Owner or owners? At first sight, we might think they are the same boot recast eight times, but closer inspection reveals that each is unique. The monotony of manufacture, with its repeated actions to produce replicated objects, is transformed by the use to which the objects are put. The commonplace objects become charged with the individuality of having different owners. The ordinary becomes the extraordinary. The identical becomes unique.

*Natalie Luckyj, *Other Realities: The Legacy of Surrealism in Canadian Art* (Kingston: Agnes Etherington Art Centre, 1978), p.17.

Gathie Falk
Herd Two (1975),
plywood with pencil and eraser over white enamel paint,
2.5 × 5.0 m installation space;
each horse 79.0 × 125.0 × 1.9 cm (approx.).
National Gallery of Canada.

Gathie Falk
Eight Red Boots (1973),
red-glazed ceramic in painted plywood and glass cabinet,
101.2 × 105.7 × 15.5 cm; each ceramic boot,
17.0 × 28.0 × 10.0 cm (approx.).
Purchase, 1974.
Accession No. 18157.

Royden Rabinowitch

born 1943

Sculpture has become an open term. The word is now used as much to describe a broad set of activities as to define a particular class of objects. In much of this new work, the very notion of sculpture has been shifted from the viewer's concentration on an object to the viewer's experience around the object. Too often, this has resulted in vagueness of purpose, a stuttering narrative or quasi-theatricality. Royden Rabinowitch has described how a sculpture that disposes a wide range of views is not the same as one that can be examined from a variety of viewpoints. But against the scattering of experience, he has brought to his work a disciplined focus on the issues of our perception of the world. Through this, we come to recognize space not as a limitless void partially filled with objects but as the dimension of our lived experience; we construct space by the range of our activities.

The *Nine Right Limits Added to a Piecewise Linear Developed Five Manifold with Three Ground Planes* of 1977 is one of an extensive series of steel floor sculptures that Rabinowitch has made. The title is a description of the particular construction of the work, revealing that the process within the sculpture is one that moves from a general experience to specific sensations. First, there is the manifold, a steel plate cut to a chosen shape and bent around various axes to produce a form that is in contact with the ground along some of its edges and elsewhere is raised up from it. To this a number of steel plates are welded, giving specific definition to the manifold to which they have been added. The title also describes the work when viewed from a particular place. When standing at the highest point of the sculpture, the thickest of the nine "limits" (the plates added to the manifold) are on the right. As we move around

the sculpture, so our perception of the work and the relationship between the manifold and its limits is altered and expanded. The complexity of the sculpture, disposing a multiplicity of viewpoints, arises from the construction being asymmetrical about all its axes.

Rabinowitch has written about the construction of the sculptures in general terms saying, "Limiting a manifold seems to be the ordinary way I proceed in the world. Whole experience, i.e. the manifold, comes first; reflection on and memory of the experience, i.e. additions to the manifold, come afterwards."*

The sculpture exists as a rigorous and concentrated model of the way in which we perceive the world. By our activities, our memories, and our associations, we organize our changing viewpoints in time and space. By concentrating on a very specific and precisely developed object, Rabinowitch leads us to recognize the complexity of how we relate to the world, proceeding not from a fixed point but through our dynamic lived experience.

* *10 Canadian Artists in the 1970s* (Toronto: Art Gallery of Ontario, 1980), p.88.

Royden Rabinowitch
*Nine Right Limits Added to a Piecewise Linear Developed Five
Manifold with Three Ground Planes* (1977),
steel, 4.0 × 273.6 × 47.5 cm.
Purchase, 1979.
Accession No. 23400.

David Rabinowitch

born 1943

With sculpture in the classical tradition, the viewer is drawn around the object in a seamless transition from one vantage point to the next. Baroque sculpture, more theatrical in effect, depends on a principal viewing point and on secondary views which often offer surprising changes. In both cases, the sense of the sculpture resides imaginatively within its core. These characteristics have persisted into our own time, even though the character, style, and iconography of sculpture may have changed beyond all recognition.

David Rabinowitch has radically recast the fundamental approach both to the object and to the viewing of sculpture. Reversing the notion of sculpture as an object principally built up in the vertical dimension, his work has invariably been horizontal and set directly on the floor or the ground.

Through the 1970s, he made a series of sculptures grouped under the designation "Romanesque." The National Gallery's piece, the third in the series, is *Metrical (Romanesque) Constructions in 5 Masses and 2 Scales, No. 2*. The sculptures were all made from solid mild steel and each has five contiguous elements, the masses, which are distinct in size and shape (the exception being the second in the series which has only three masses). In three or four of the masses of each sculpture, holes have been bored through the thickness of the steel, the diameters of the bores varying to form different scales. In the National Gallery work, the holes are of two different sizes, the "2 Scales." With the thickness of the steel ranging from around five centimetres in some of the works to as much as fifteen centimetres in the largest, the sculptures are very heavy, but their massive physical properties contrast with the purely visual character by which we perceive them.

The sculptures embody a complex set of interrelated measures and relationships: their overall horizontal shape; the shapes of the individual masses; the thickness and vertical dimensions; and the interlocking rhythm formed by the different sizes and patterns of the bored holes in relation to the individual masses and the overall shape. However, this description is vastly different from what the viewer who moves around the work experiences. Although from any particular vantage point we can encompass the whole shape and distinguish its individual parts, every viewpoint offers a totally different version of the shape, as well as presenting distinct rhythms in the relationship between the masses and the reading of the scales. At each point we carry a concept of the whole and revise it, seeking to recognize from every viewpoint what we know to be true—that the masses are stable and unchanging, and the scales fixed.

The sense of the core in traditional sculpture is eliminated, and with it the notion of an ideal point of view. Here, what can be agreed upon is a descriptive catalogue of what is physically present, but interpretation is shifted outside the sculpture—to the movement of the viewer around it and to the subjective experience of perceiving and continually reconstructing the reality of the object.

David Rabinowitch
*Metrical (Romanesque) Constructions in 5 Masses and 2 Scales,
No. 2* (1975–76),
hot-rolled steel, 5.3 × 205.0 × 175.9 cm.
Purchase, 1976.
Accession No. 18680.

Ron Martin

born 1943

Ron Martin was one of the young artists from London, Ontario, who was included in the seminal National Gallery exhibition, "The Heart of London." When he first showed his *World Paintings* in 1971, he said, "I'd like to feel I could make a painting that is primarily about the experience of the experiencer." The statement has a particular edge to it, for while our immediate assumption is that this refers to the address the work makes to us as viewers, it can just as well apply to the artist himself. He is, after all, not excluded from being an experiencer, even of his own work. The statement is charged all the more by the fact that with the *World Paintings*, as with Martin's subsequent series of works, he has sought to avoid the determined expressionism and formalism that stand as justification for so much abstract painting. If we look for a meaning by analysing the surfaces of Martin's paintings, we shall simply be frustrated.

The *World Paintings* form a distinct, finite series. They were made in 1970 and consist of thirty-nine paintings. All except one are identical in size, and all are built up through a common surface structure. The National Gallery painting, *World No. 33*, is one of the most visually complex because of the number of colours used. The system by which the paintings are made is as follows: on each one-inch square section of the canvas, there are three short strokes of colour, the strokes running vertically in one square, horizontally in the next. The colours in the squares run through the scale of possible combinations. The system is such that the individual square units form larger clusters interlocked horizontally, vertically, and diagonally.

At first, perhaps, conscientiously seeking to retrace the artist's steps, we may attempt to discern the underlying pattern, stepping back to discover how it operates on the overall scale. But our efforts will not be rewarded.

Moreover, as we step back, we find that the individuality of detail begins to transform into a shifting total experience as our eyes mix the colours optically. And rather than being able to define a fixed pattern, we begin to recognize that the only dependable pattern is the one we form in shifting our attention from one part of the canvas to another. With no solution making itself evident either through formal analysis or through expressiveness, we must return to the statement about "the experience of the experiencer"; that is, we must recognize the experience of the painting as a phenomenon, before attempting any analysis or rationalization.

In subsequent series of paintings, the *One-Colour Paintings* and the *Black Paintings*, Martin restricted his use of colour and applied the paint with broad sweeping gestures. While our responses to these paintings, visually, physically, and emotionally, will differ from those towards the *World Paintings*, the purpose remains the same. The phenomenon that is each particular painting is unchanged.

The difficulty in Martin's painting—and its integrity—is the extent to which it brings the viewer immediately in contact with his or her own experience. The mediating factors that we traditionally attach to painting are suspended. The desire for some underlying meaning, some solution that will explain our pleasure or our discomfort, is not satisfied, as it cannot be satisfied. That, as always, is the difficulty.

Ron Martin
World No. 33 (1970),
acrylic and graphite on canvas, 214.0 × 153.0 cm.
Purchase, 1971.
Accession No. 16722.

213

Colette Whiten

born 1945

Taking casts from the human body seems an obvious way of making figurative sculpture, but it raises problems, for it narrows the boundary between art and life. The issues involved may test our assumptions about the practice of art making and the grounds for our aesthetic judgements. Equally, they may absolve us of responsibility, allowing us to settle for the kitsch of the waxworks, where the lifelike is merely the lifeless.

A number of sculptors from the 1950s began using casts, challenging art and its practices. The pluralization of interests led to widely differing results. George Segal, for instance, made white plaster figures as participants in complex installations; his *Gas Station* of 1963 (National Gallery) is an example. Duane Hanson and John d'Andrea have used fibreglass and other materials to produce *trompe-l'oeil* figures that unnervingly shift the waxworks tableaux from their theatrical presentation of the famous into the anonymity of the everyday.

Colette Whiten's cast sculptures move in yet another direction. When Whiten began to work in the early 1970s, her sculptures were often compared to those of George Segal, but the comparison is misleading. Segal's works are suspended narratives of banal situations; he was concerned with selecting and freezing "the gestures that are most telling." Whiten's works deny narrative, and her earliest pieces were as much concerned with the process of their production as with the results of the castings.

The most ambitious of her early sculptures was *Structure No. 8* of 1972 (Art Gallery of Ontario). She built a wood and metal device with spaces for four people to stand, their arms outstretched, their fingertips touching.

With the people held in this way, she made casts from them in fibreglass. The wood structure is reminiscent of the medieval punishment stocks (other works she made at this time also look like crude torture machines). The work, however, is not only the wood structure and the casts; it also includes the process of the work, documented on film and in photographs. The impersonality of the structure, with its connotations of victimization, contrasts with the casts of the people as individuals and the reality of the sensitive process which was recorded on film.

A few years later, in *September 1975*, Whiten made a group of structures in which the casts and casting devices were united. Here, the record of each person is preserved in a hinged "mummy case" which consists of two sections, one with a cast of the person's front and one of the back. The images obtained are precise and detailed, and each presents a powerful visual ambiguity. From any distance, it seems that we are looking at a figure in relief. As we move closer, we see that the image is deeply recessed. It is an ambiguity between an impression and an expression—a strong sense of human presence, though we know that the figure is absent. The values of Whiten's sculptures lie in their sensitivity towards individuals. While the forms of the "mummy cases" are like the broad conventions we use to form and mould our generalized images of people, the casts inside them define particular individuals.

Colette Whiten
September 1975 (1975),
plaster, burlap, wood, rope, fibreglass, metal, paint; male
figure, 232.0 × 152.0 × 85.5 cm; smaller male figure,
227.5 × 145.0 × 85.0 cm; female figure, 209.0 × 134.4 × 83.0 cm.
Purchase, 1976.
Accession No. 18549.

John McEwen

born 1945

In relation to his sculpture *Model*, John McEwen wrote the following riddle:

A model after the fact (the grindstone came first)
An equation but not an equals sign
A three-dimensional word to stand in for intent
An attempt to grasp the past
The link between my left and right hand
The realization of being here*

The lines form a series of contrasts, or tensions, substantiated by the final "The realization of being here." They parallel the form of the sculpture, which consists of three linked but disparate elements: a grindstone; a steel disc; and the letters MODEL mounted on the wall between the first two elements. The grindstone is a "ready-made," a surviving piece of industrial machinery. The wheel attached to it is to accommodate a drive-belt to link it to a power source. The steel disc corresponds to the grindstone, forming a sort of counterbalance to it; but unlike the stone, its practical purpose is obscure. Not only is it difficult to understand what assembly the disc might fit into, but its weight and sealed shape and the way it lies flat on the ground denies ease of movement, contrasting with the suspension of the stone. Further, in the centre of the disc, where we might expect to find the hole drilled for a spindle, there is the outline of a bird cut through the thickness of the steel. The letters MODEL are also formed from steel. Attached to the wall, they assert a self-evident meaning, as well as linking the two other elements as if by way of designation and explanation.

Pluralities 1980 (Ottawa: National Gallery, 1980), p.85.

In the early 1970s, McEwen was involved with that broad range of activity gathered under the term Conceptual Art. "In Conceptual Art," the American critic John Perrault wrote in 1971, "the idea is paramount and the materials are immaterial. Well, almost." In the course of the 1970s, McEwen worked with situations that can be called the "equation that was not an equals sign," situations that press on the links we make between abstract notions and their physical manifestations.

The key to *Model* seems to lie within the word, yet the enigma remains in the multiplicity of definitions: model as the original form of something; as a replica; as a standard; as a means of display—the artist's model. Similarly, the grindstone is at the centre of a complex that shifts from being a practical object to being a reference to past industrial practices, and to standing as a metaphor—"keeping one's nose to the grindstone." These tensions are extended by the apparent contradiction of the ground-hugging steel disc and the shape of a bird extracted from it. What is "the link between my left and right hand" if it is not myself? Just as I am the link between my rational and intuitive faculties.

John McEwen
Model (1978–79),
grindstone, steel disc, and steel letters; grindstone,
109.2 × 88.3 cm; steel disc, 70.0 cm diameter × 5.1 cm
thick; steel letters (each), 9.5 × 1.9 cm.
Purchase, 1981.
Accession No. 23897.

General Idea

group formed 1968

It is ironic but appropriate that the conventions we use to describe and discuss art seem foolish when they are invoked to approach the work of General Idea. Ironic and appropriate, because the wide range of General Idea's projects are and have been a continual return on convention. Not only has this range removed them from the simple categories for ordering discussion, but the very fact of their continuing production of work adds to their art history, rooting the group's present activities all the more firmly into the structure of their own making.

The group, which was formed in 1968, consists of three people known under their pseudonyms of A. A. Bronson, Felix Partz, and Jorge Zontal. The very name of the group, General Idea, combines both the sense of authority and the broad meaning of "catching on": "We wanted to be famous; we wanted to be glamorous; we wanted to be rich. That is to say, we wanted to be artists, and we knew that if we were famous, if we were glamorous, we could say, we are artists and we would be."*

The group organized a series of events centring on the Miss General Idea beauty contest. After "The 1971 Miss General Idea Pageant," held at the Art Gallery of Ontario, they set 1984 as the date for the next pageant and over the following thirteen years set to work towards that event. As they stated in their catalogue, "Miss General Idea of 1984 is basically this: an ideal framing device for arresting attention without throwing away the key." The preparations involved bringing Culture into culture, or culture into Culture and, more specifically, of projecting into the future while assembling an archaeology of the present. They communicated the progress of these preparations through *File*

magazine, which they founded in 1972, having based its appearance and its mixture of text and photographs on *Life* magazine.

Most importantly, the preparations towards 1984 included the moves that would see the construction of the *Miss General Idea 1984 Pavilion*, as well as preparing for its destruction and reconstruction. Hence, *Reconstructing Futures* appeared in 1977, an installation containing elements from the pavilion and, on the walls, large-scale photographs of the plans for the ziggurat-shaped building and its burning and destruction. On the back wall, behind the screen, is a photograph of the distraught members of the group, their faces blackened by smoke, escaping the disaster.

Over the following years, sections and fragments of the pavilion began to appear—its *Boutique* and the *Colour Bar Lounge* among others, as well as paintings and surviving pieces of decoration. In a series of exhibitions held in museums and galleries, these fragments were reassembled, culminating in a retrospective exhibition held in 1984–85, which was shown in Canada, the Netherlands, and Switzerland. If the pavilion was lost, the spirit of Miss General Idea was not. New manifestations of the group began to appear in 1983 and 1984 in the form of poodles and babies, accompanied by the sign of a cornucopia, the promise of plenty. The pantomorphism of General Idea is not lost but is always preparing once more to multiply.

*"Glamour," *File*, Vol.3, No.1, 1975, p.21.

General Idea
Reconstructing Futures (1977),
14 photo-montage panels, 2 vinyl-upholstered seats, 2 marble
and steel barbells, synthetic carpet, 2 copper and metal-
plated lamps, 6 perforated steel panels, recorded soundtrack,
tape recorder, 4 fluorescent light tubes, 2.74 × 4.32 × 10.17 m.
Purchase, 1983.
Accession No. 28286.

John Hall

born 1943

The very character of still-life painting comprises and expresses contradiction. Life is not still and the subjects of such works are usually contrived situations, constructed by the artist for the purpose of painting. This structure, however, reflects the traditional intent of still life to draw together extreme conditions—beauty and decay, life and death, the fleeting pleasures of the five senses. Such paintings are objects of contemplation, bittersweet images of the transitory facts of worldly life. The more beautiful the surface of the picture, the more poignant is the reality of loss.

John Hall is a painter of still life. But while, in traditional still life, objects were chosen from the natural world, Hall invariably chooses man-made objects; and while, in traditional still life, the boundary between painting and reality was all but dissolved, in Hall's work the painting is distanced technically by the use of photography and a style of heightened realism. Further, the objects he chooses are rarely precious. Usually banal, often tawdry, and more likely to be discarded than to decay, they hold value principally by the memories and sentiments which their owners attach to them, or by the associations which they stimulate in our experience.

Hall began making his still-life paintings in the mid-1960s, encouraged by the example of Robert Rauschenberg and American Pop Art to deal with the mass of popular cultural material which surrounds us, attaches to us, describes us, and which we use, junk, treasure, and ignore. He proceeded by first constructing the still lifes and then painting them. Through the 1970s, he built them as wall-related structures, playing on the relationship between still-life objects and still-life paintings as if they belonged to the same order of things. He heightened this tension in his works of the late 1970s by exhibiting the painting and its objective model side by side.

In the early 1970s, Hall made a number of very large-scale paintings, such as *Doll* of 1971. The objects are cheap things: a plastic doll set between a couple of plastic roses, displayed against the background of a flattened Coca-Cola box. The painting, at over four metres long, has the proportions of an advertising billboard, but its content is an ironic inversion of the purpose of advertisement, which is to create a desire for the product. Ironic, too, is the reference that the triptych shape makes to a specific tradition in the history of painting—altarpieces—in which meaning is assumed to lie behind surface appearance. Here we must deal with the inconsequence of the objects and a style of painting that thrusts attention onto the surface of things. Since the late 1970s, the surfaces of Hall's paintings have become more glitzy and more reflective. Whereas the tradition of still life was to draw us into quiet meditation, Hall attracts us with the brilliance of his surfaces and simultaneously denies them to us by their adamant hardness.

John Hall
Doll (1971),
acrylic on canvas, 162.5 × 411.5 cm overall; left panel,
162.5 × 122.1 cm; centre panel 162.5 × 162.5 cm; right panel
162.5 × 121.9 cm.
Purchase, 1972.
Accession No. 16994.

Jeff Wall

born 1946

The history of painting and photography is interwoven. Subjects popular in painting were set up and photographed, while photographs became the basis for paintings. The development of art history as a major academic subject has been inseparable from the easy availability of slides; theses can be written and degrees gained without the need to see the original works of art. While abstract art appeared to free painting from its collusion with photography (though it could not avoid being photographed), that freedom only confirmed how art had yielded its central place in visual culture to photography, film, and television.

Jeff Wall has chosen to present his images not only through photography but by a delivery system used in advertising, with large-scale cibachrome transparencies backlit by fluorescent tubes. As with advertising material, Wall's images represent contrived situations. For all their apparent spontaneity, the photographs are not candid records of fleeting moments; they are fictions, in the way that the situations of painting are fictions.

Wall develops his images through the meticulous presentation of a situation. The technical means he uses, with the strongly lit transparencies, sets us before brilliantly sharp images in which every square centimetre is fully and equally present to us. The result is at once fascinating and disturbing; the almost excruciating attention to detail compels us to believe that nothing can be overlooked. While Wall's earlier works tended to describe relatively static situations, his more recent works have emphasized dynamic situations centred on gesture, heightening the tension between our perception of a "stilled" moment and our interpretation of a lived experience. None of the works, however, are inseparable from the interweaving of other images and references. Wall once wrote, "Pictures in the art context are necessarily open to, and constructed out of, elements, texts, or readings generated across the horizon of common or popular as well as academic forms of literacy."*

*"To the Spectator," *Jeff Wall: Installation of Faking Death (1977), The Destroyed Room (1978), Young Workers (1979), Picture for Women (1979)* (Victoria: Art Gallery of Greater Victoria, 1979).

The Destroyed Room is horrifying in its evidence of violence. This is mediated by the way that the situation is "constructed" in a similar way to a film set. Yet we cannot disengage ourselves from transferring the evidence of violence from the inert objects to the possible occupant of the room. We find ourselves looking for traces of her—for the victim of this assault is surely a woman. The only object in the room not subject to destruction or violation is the figurine of a curtseying dancer, which introduces an ironic and pathetic sentiment of innocence. In the essay Wall wrote when this work was first shown, he illustrated it with four comparative photographs. One showed the studio containing the "set"; one was a snapshot of a shop window in Paris filled with trinkets; the other two were works of art—a detail from Marcel Duchamp's *Given 1. The Waterfall 2. The Illuminating Gas*, 1944–66, and Eugène Delacroix's *The Death of Sardanapalus*, 1827. Both of these images, which are at very different ends of the artistic spectrum, combine violence and the erotic. They construct a partial context for *The Destroyed Room*, opening its layers of visual reference to the social and psychological readings of each of us, from our own experience (I myself, for instance, am reminded of Picasso's *Guernica*). The image raises taut questions by its links between the lasting meaning of art and the immediate, appalling commonplace of unconscionable violence.

Jeff Wall
The Destroyed Room (1978),
cibachrome transparency in fluorescent light box,
179.0 × 249.0 × 20.6 cm.
Purchase, 1979.
Accession No. 23401.

Liz Magor

born 1948

Liz Magor's *Production* is the record of a process, an outcome of the interaction between what is individual and subjective on the one hand and, on the other, what is mechanical and impersonal. It is the process of change in which what we initiate as individuals both reflects our independence and in turn moulds and transforms us. Magor once wrote, "While I use this work to make manifest some aspects of a personal history, I find I have simultaneously manufactured my own competition as the pieces themselves take the opportunity to manifest *their* history, their own generation and transformation."*

Production consists of two distinct but interdependent parts. The first is a wooden mechanical device: a press and four rectangular moulds. The second is the product made with that device: thousands of bricks. Magor made the bricks from newspapers, which she soaked, mushed into a pulp, and then compressed in the moulds. There is a timeless character to the appearance of the piece—an early, simple machine powered only by the repetitive physical actions of the operator. The final work can be displayed in various configurations. Its installation at the National Gallery is particularly striking, with the bricks appearing to form part of the building's structure and with the mould device set in front of the wall, implying that the process is a continuing one.

The tradition of fine art has centred—and largely continues to centre—on the individual artist producing unique objects. Magor casts doubt on this tradition by dedicating herself to a form of mass production and by using as her materials a product of the mass media. Yet her work, conceptually and physically, is individual work, just as the stories in the newspapers are drawn on the lives of individuals. And as her work is subsumed and transformed in the impersonality of mass production, so the lives of the people involved in the events reported in the newspapers are subsumed and transformed in the impersonality of mass communication.

Despite the mass-produced character of the work and the mass-media treatment that newspapers express, the individuality of Magor's work and of the people whose stories are told are not lost. They are preserved in the bricks. The irony in this is how her activity, as an individual, transforms the ephemeral products of the mass news media into a form that is associated with stability and endurance.

The level of irony is redoubled by the way that, for all the repetitive indifference in the production of the bricks, Magor's artistic process does give a particular character in texture and colour to each of the bricks. For although we are faced with a mass of similar objects, identically produced, their appearance is not uniform. It is a matter of distance and point of view, just as it is to recognize that a crowd is composed of individual people. The extraordinary strength of *Production* lies in the way that the more we consider it, the more it reveals about the endless process of formation and transformation between the mass and the individual. We assert our individuality, we insist upon it—and yet we cannot escape the physical, psychological, and cultural moulds from which we are made.

*Liz Magor: *Production/Reproduction* (Vancouver: Vancouver Art Gallery, 1980).

Liz Magor
Production (1980),
newspaper, wood, steel, machine, 134.6 × 81.3 × 61.0 cm;
paper bricks: 5.1 × 10.2 × 20.3 cm each.
Purchase, 1984.
Accession No. 28453.

Joanne Tod

born 1953

Painting—and not exclusively representational painting—reaches ironically over two assumptions. The first is that although painting is an art on the surface, its meaning must lie elsewhere, deep beneath appearances. The second is the way that the images of painting, despite the infinite possibilities of their appearance and interpretation, are accepted as natural, reflecting neutral, broadly accepted values. The irony is that so much twentieth-century art, even in setting out to challenge these assumptions, has had its assertions of opposition and dissent co-opted.

The subtlety of Joanne Tod's work is that its confrontation of these assumptions undermines them from within. In the first place, she is a very good painter, controlling very large surfaces, and doing so with a technical range that allows her to shift the mood, the character, and the address of her pictures. Her subversion is all the more effective because of its transparency, slipping past the criticism that she is unable to emulate what she challenges. She accepts the pre-eminence of the surface and reinforces this by the way that she derives her images, directly or indirectly, from photographs. Photographs are invariably overdetermined, and the more candid and more natural they appear, the broader is the range of interpretation to which they are susceptible. Tod works with this ambiguity, this capacity for layering the surfaces of appearance, countering and recountering the "naturalness" of situations.

In many of her pictures, Tod has used and then disrupted the aspects of security and stability on which Western society is based—material wealth, big business, the tradition of art, the assumed role of women, the institution of the church—revealing the relativity of these structures, both in their vulnerability and their resistance to change. So often, the stark directness of her images seem first to affirm the reality of a situation (at least, the reality that we recognize from newspaper or magazine photographs) and then, by a satirical twist or an incongruous juxtaposition of elements, to destroy it. The irony is the extent to which we come to recognize how her presentation of the surface of things does represent reality to us.

Having Fun? The Time of Our Lives is a work in two parts. Both images refer to theatrical events, though at differing ends of the cultural spectrum: the one a scene from a ballet; the other perhaps a cabaret night at a social club, or the evening entertainment at a cheap holiday resort. No audience is shown in the ballet scene. There does not have to be an audience because, whether or not we are ballet enthusiasts, we like to think of ourselves, socially and culturally, as being there. Quite the opposite is true of the cabaret scene. In it, we are shown members of the audience precisely so that we can disassociate ourselves from them. Both pictures centre on the gestures of the women dancers. The ballerina displays the typical affected gestures of mock resistance and coy compliance to seduction. Yet although the conventionality of the gestures and the artistic context of the ballet distance the situation from reality, they secretly affirm a sense of naturalness. The cabaret dancer, however, is right among the audience, "as large as life," her gestures aggressive and obvious. The relationship between her and her audience is charged with racial overtones and blurred between fantasy and reality. But as we look from one picture to the other, distinguishing between them, the closer we must come to recognize that those distinctions are less of substance than of convention. The longer we stand in front of them, the closer together they come, like the two images of a stereograph which we resolve into a single lifelike picture.

Joanne Tod
Having Fun? The Time of our Lives (1984),
oil on canvas, two panels, each 199.0 × 199.0 cm.
Purchase, 1985.
Accession No. 28717.2; 28717.1.

Index

Acknowledgements

It has been a pleasure and a privilege for me to write about works of art in the National Gallery of Canada collections. The pleasure is all the greater because, having come to know many of the works when they were hung in the Lorne Building, I was able to see them afresh in their superb new surroundings.

My work has been made possible because of the interest and support of many people at the National Gallery. I would like to thank in particular Dr. Shirley L. Thomson, Director, for her immediate reception of the idea for this book and for her support and guidance in the stages of its preparation. I am also greatly indebted for the assistance and advice I have received from Charles C. Hill, Curator of Canadian Art, and Rosemarie Tovell, Curator of Canadian Prints and Drawings. My thanks also go to Yves Dagenais, Deputy Director, Susan Campbell, Chief, Reproductive Services and Sales, and Greg Spurgeon, Collections Documentation Manager.

My wife Marilyn has worked with me on this project from start to finish. As always, this book is as much hers as mine.

David Burnett,
Toronto, March 1990